Accelerate:

Planes, Trains, Automobiles, and Boats!

Presented by:

Photographer's Playground

Written by: Rochelle Sibaja, Charlene Sibaja, Lynn Murphy & Roger Sibaja

Accelerate: Planes, Trains, Automobiles, and Boats!

Published by Golden Orb Business Management & Consulting

P.O Box 601

Tyrone, GA 30290

Cover concept and design, illustration, typography and photographs by Photographer's Playground Members

Printed in the United States of America

October 2018

Disclaimer: The purpose of this book is share images. It is not intended to be a historically accurate account of events or places.

ISBN 978-1-948479-01-1

Library of Congress Control Number: 2018911583

Table of Contents

About the Book

Have you ever thought to yourself, I really need to get started and do something different to grow? That was the original idea behind creating the Photographer's Playground book, Accelerate: Planes, Trains, Automobiles, and Boats. It was birthed out of the desire to collaborate with fellow photographers and create a themed body of work to accelerate involvement in the community and in photography. This book is the first collaborative project of the Photographer's Playground. Photographer's Playground is a small group of photographers of varying skills that work together to tell a story and share it with the community. Many of the photographs found in this book were taken while the group members volunteered as photographers to support local charities or events.

Planes

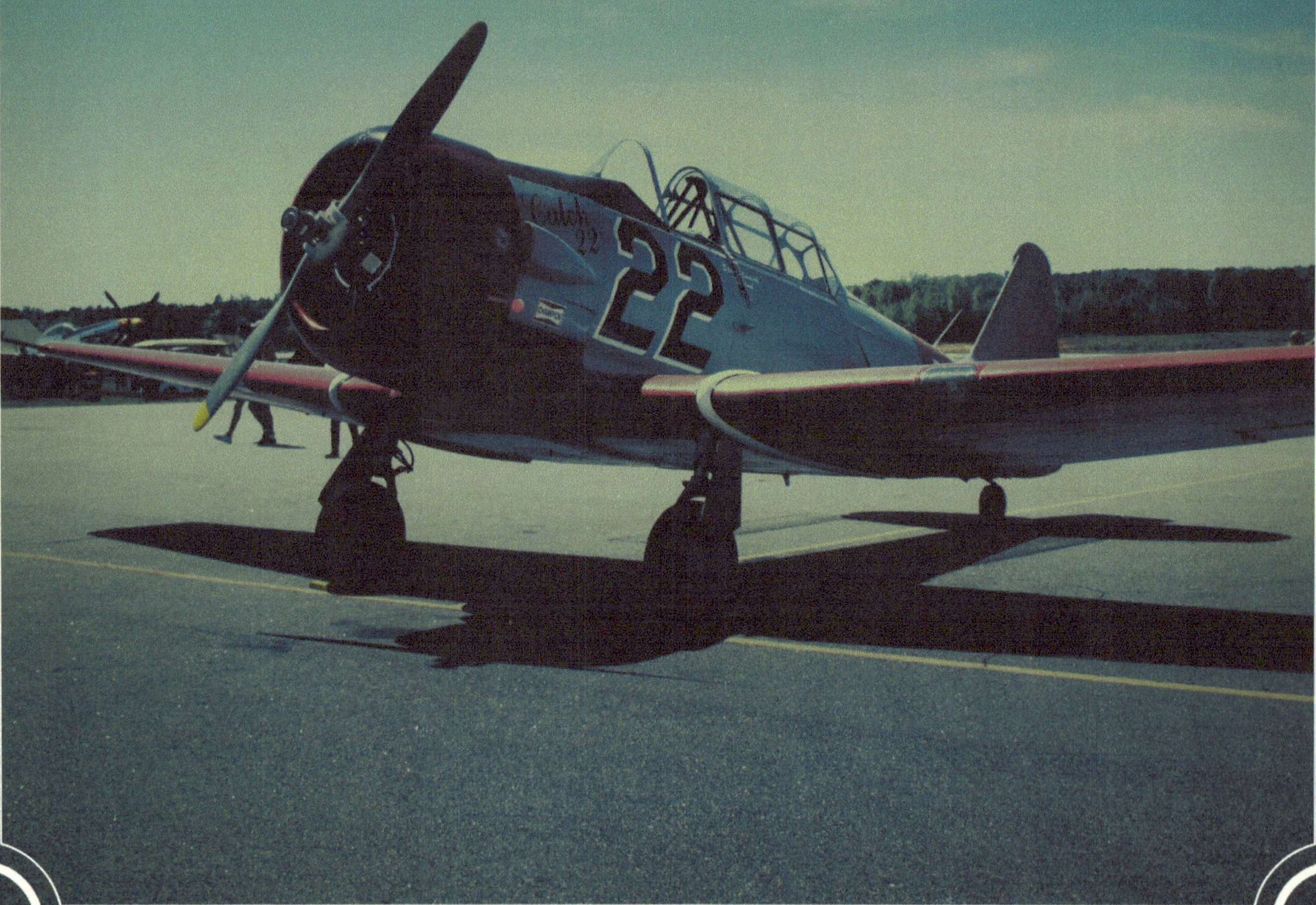

Photo by Charlene Sibaja

Planes

One of humanity's oldest dreams is the dream to fly. A shared dream that transcends space and time. Over a millennium, humans imagined soaring high to reach the sky and to touch the stars. Mythology telling tales of humans that gained the ability of flight can be found from as far back as ancient times across the world. The most famous being the Greek tale of Icarus, the man that flew too close to the sun. As time passed, humans began to create blueprints in an attempt to make their dream a reality.

A monk in the middle ages named Roger Bacon, also known as Doctor Mirabilis (Latin for "The Wonderful Teacher"), created designs for a flying mechanism that used flapping wings to fly; similarly, the famous artist and genius Leonardo Da Vinci also secretly created a design of a flying apparatus that used the flapping of wings to fly. This machine would later be named the ornithopter. Though the design was inspired, the ornithopter of that time was not stable to fly; moreover, just to get off the ground, the flapping speed was near impossible to obtain.

When people began using stable wings, the ornithopter was finally able to get airborne. Though the ornithopter was one the more older aviation designs, some people are still trying to redesign it for stable, sustainable flight. In fact, in 2010, Todd Reichert used an engineless ornithopter, the Snowbird, to stayed aloft. The Snowbird was able to fly for 476 ft in Ontario, Canada.

Sir George Cayley, dubbed the Father of Aviation, was the man who was able to pinpoint and name the forces of flight-- weight, lift, drag, and thrust. Cayley is the one to thank for the modern design of planes with fixed wings with a separate system for lift, propulsion, and control. His research and experimentation led to the first flight of a fixed-wing glider.

Later in the 1890s, Hiram Maxim created a plane that was powered by a light steam engine that was able to briefly be aloft. Maxim realized that planes require an internal-combustion, though he never attempted to create one. Maxim did, however, create an amusement park attraction that simulated what it was like to fly. He did this to gain both attention and funding.

Hiram's attraction was name Sir Hiram's Captive Flying Machines and was present in several amusement parks. Though it was a hit when introduced in 1904, over the years many of Hiram's amusement ride were decommissioned. One of his rides still is running at Blackpool Pleasure Beach in England. The ride celebrated its 110th birthday in 2014 and is the oldest theme park ride in Europe.

Otto Lilienthal designed and built gliders, and between 1891 and 1896, he completed about 2,000 flights in at least 16 different types of gliders. He was immortalized in photographs, and photos of him and his gliders circulated around the world, including the United States of America, where two brothers were intrigued with his work and findings.

When Lilienthal died due to his injuries from crashing one of his gliders, the two brother Wilbur and Orville were more determined to create a design for sustainable flight. They used aerodynamic surfaces to control an airplane in flight; leading to the very first controlled, sustained, powered flights on December 17, 1903, and began a new era of transportation.

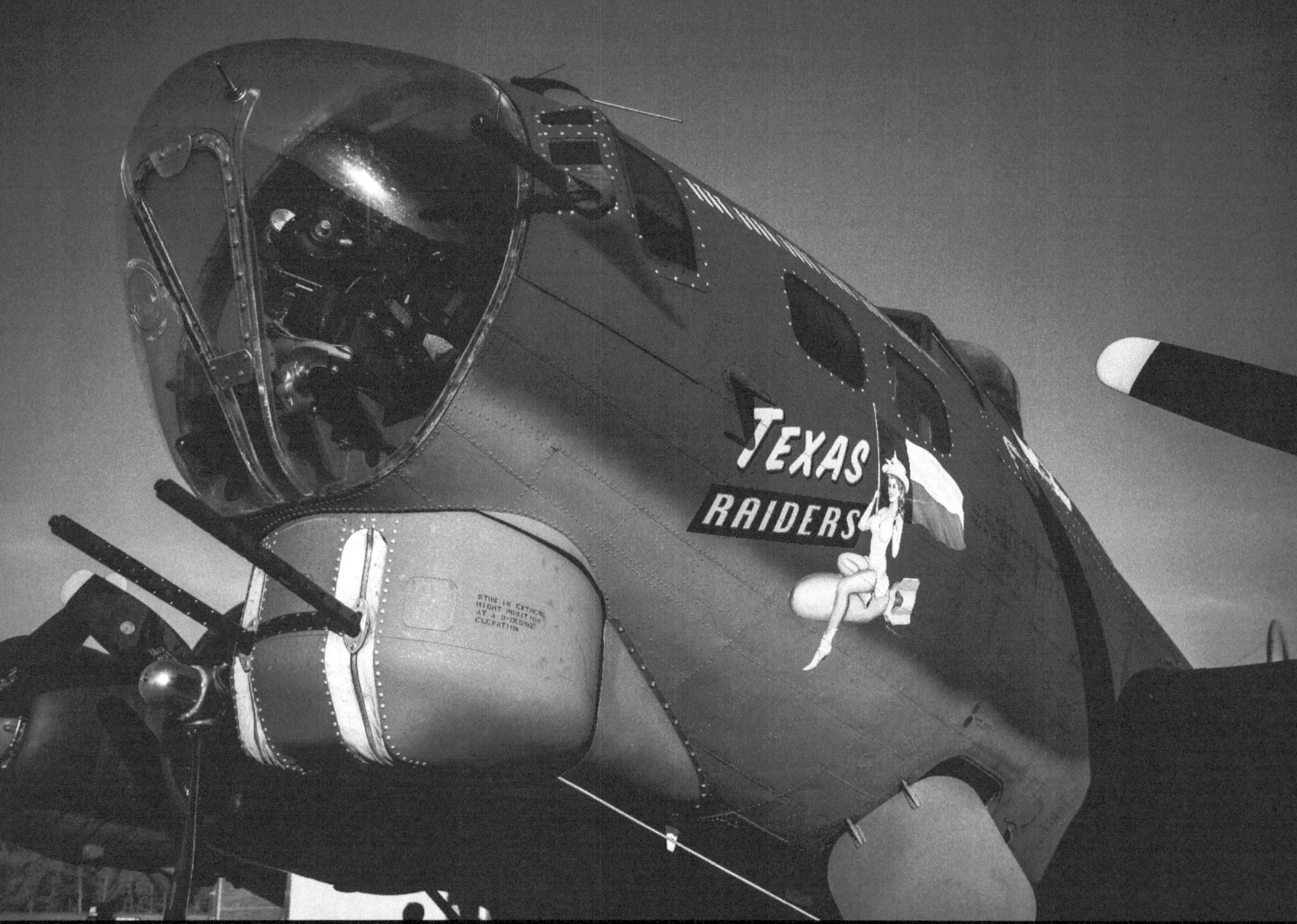

Photo by Roger Sibaja

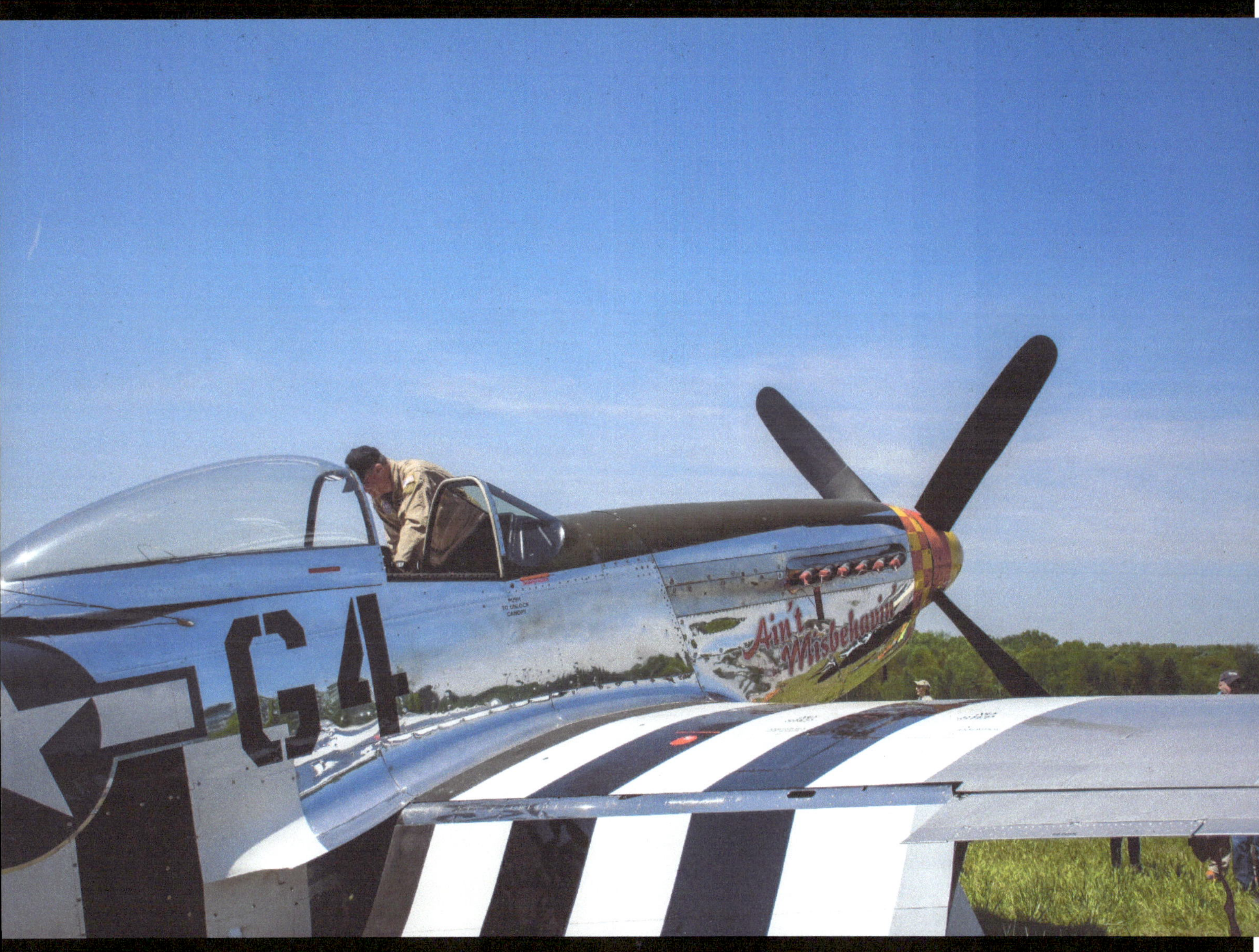

Photo by Charlene Sibaja

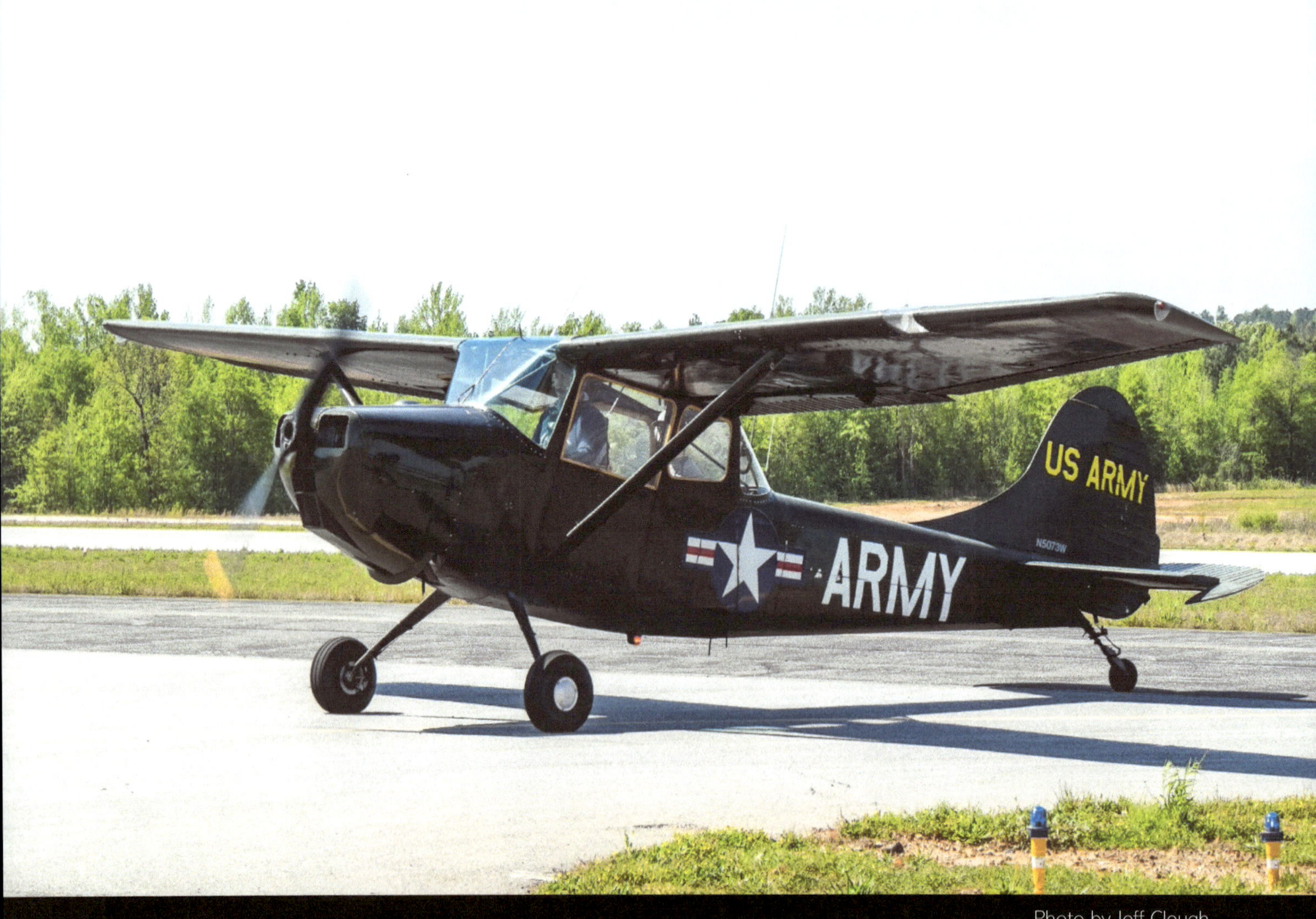

Photo by Jeff Clough

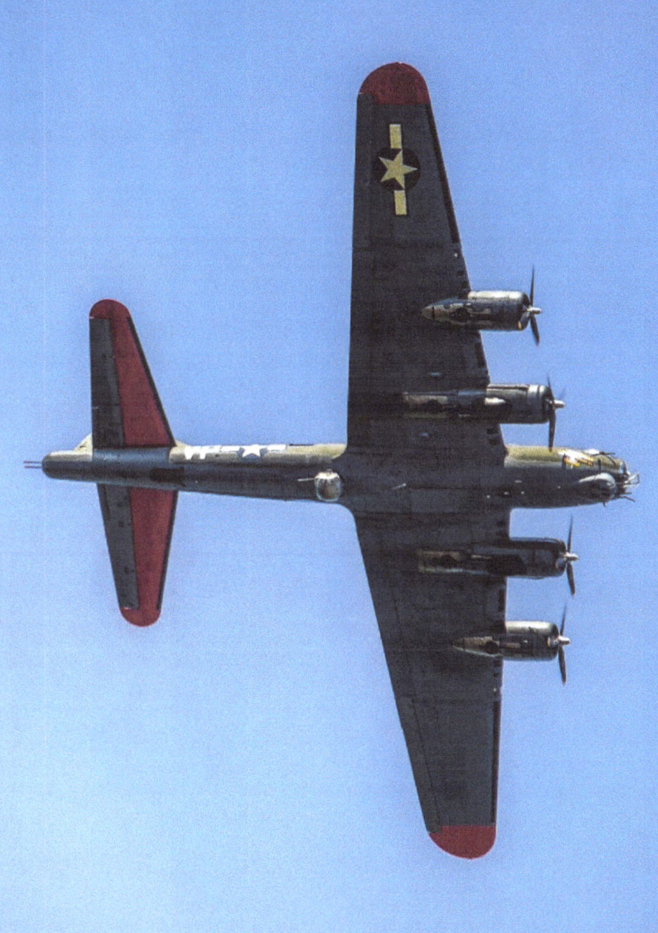

Photo by Roger Sibaja

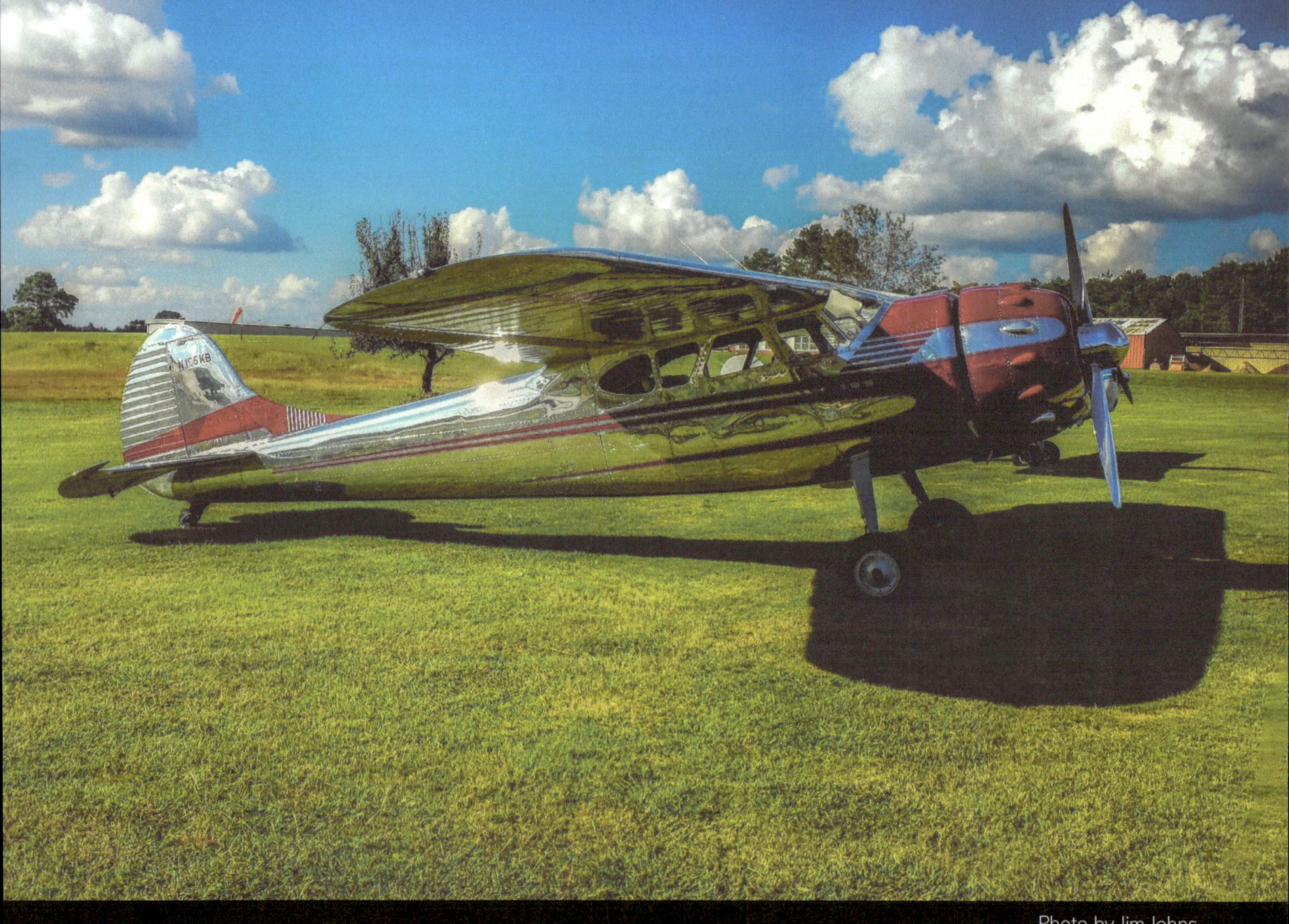

Photo by Jim Johns

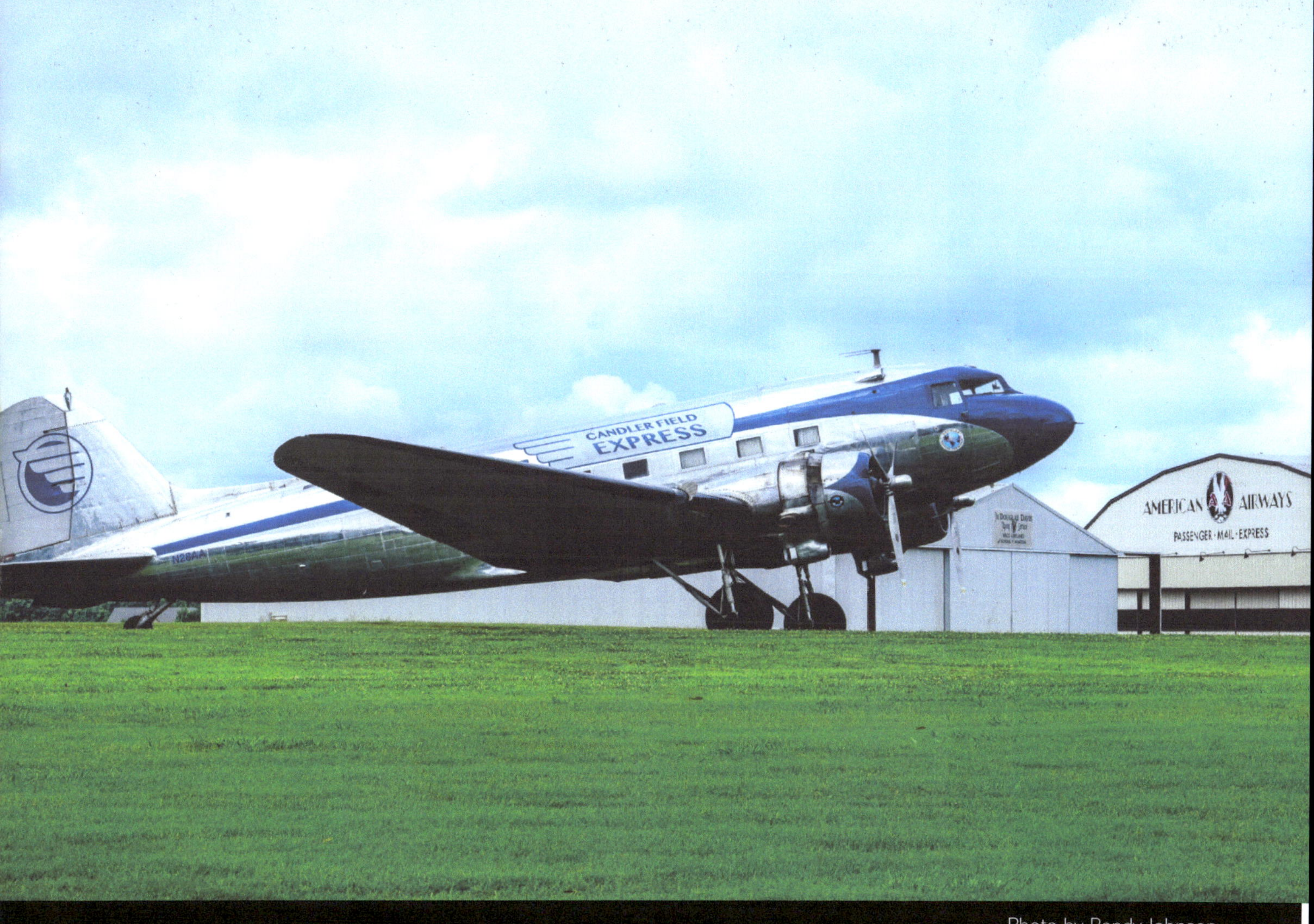

Photo by Randy Johnson

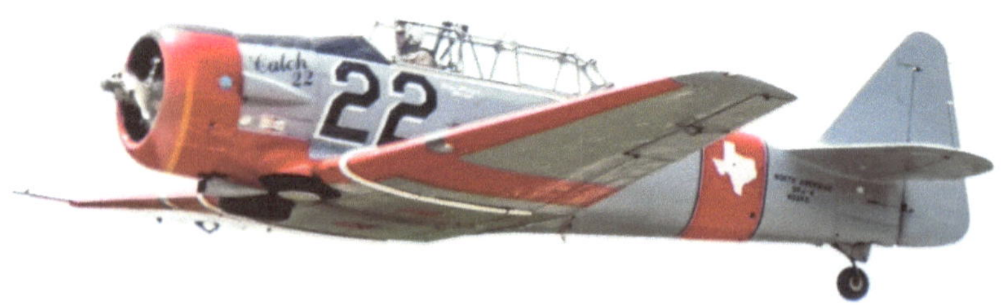

Photo Jeff Clough

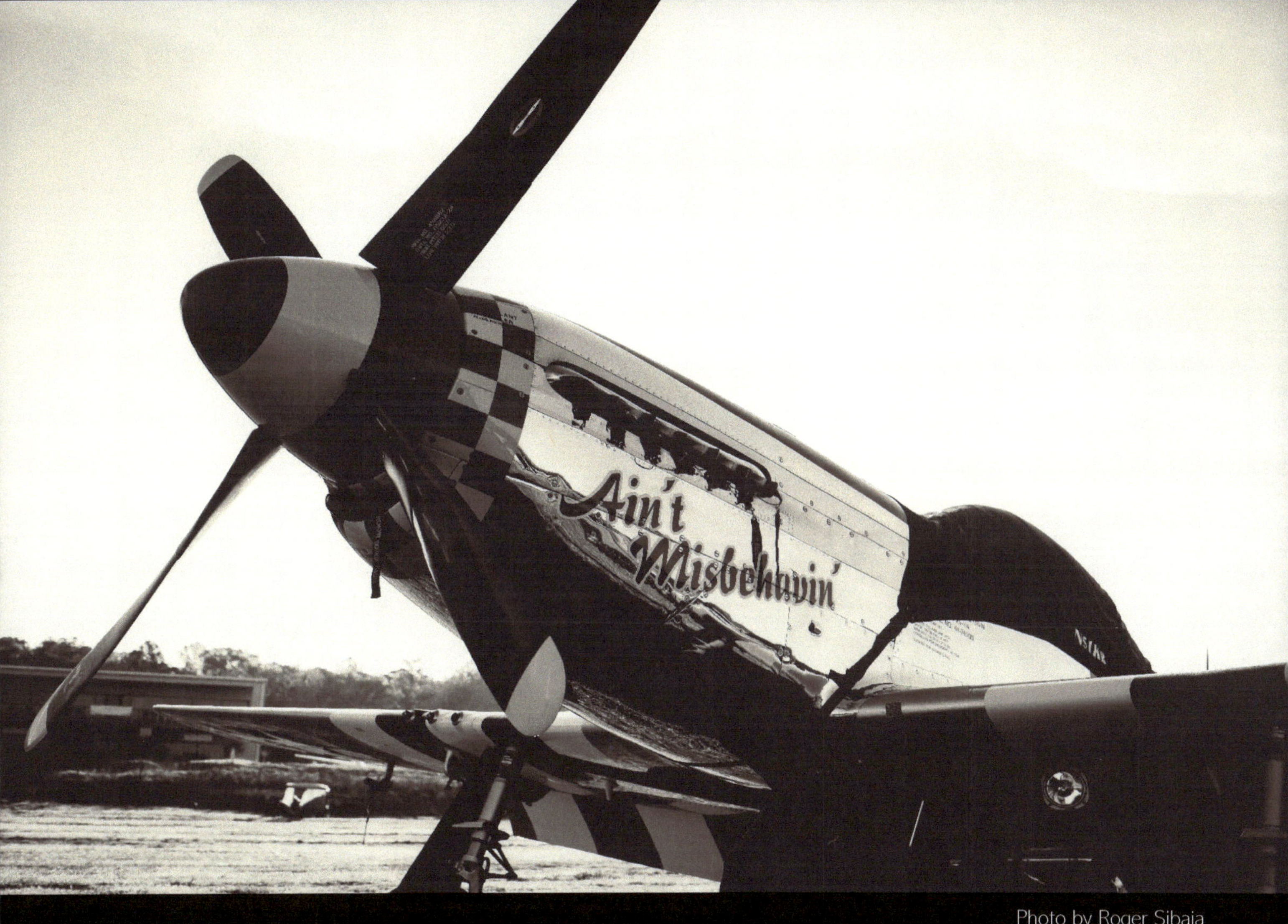

Photo by Roger Sibaja

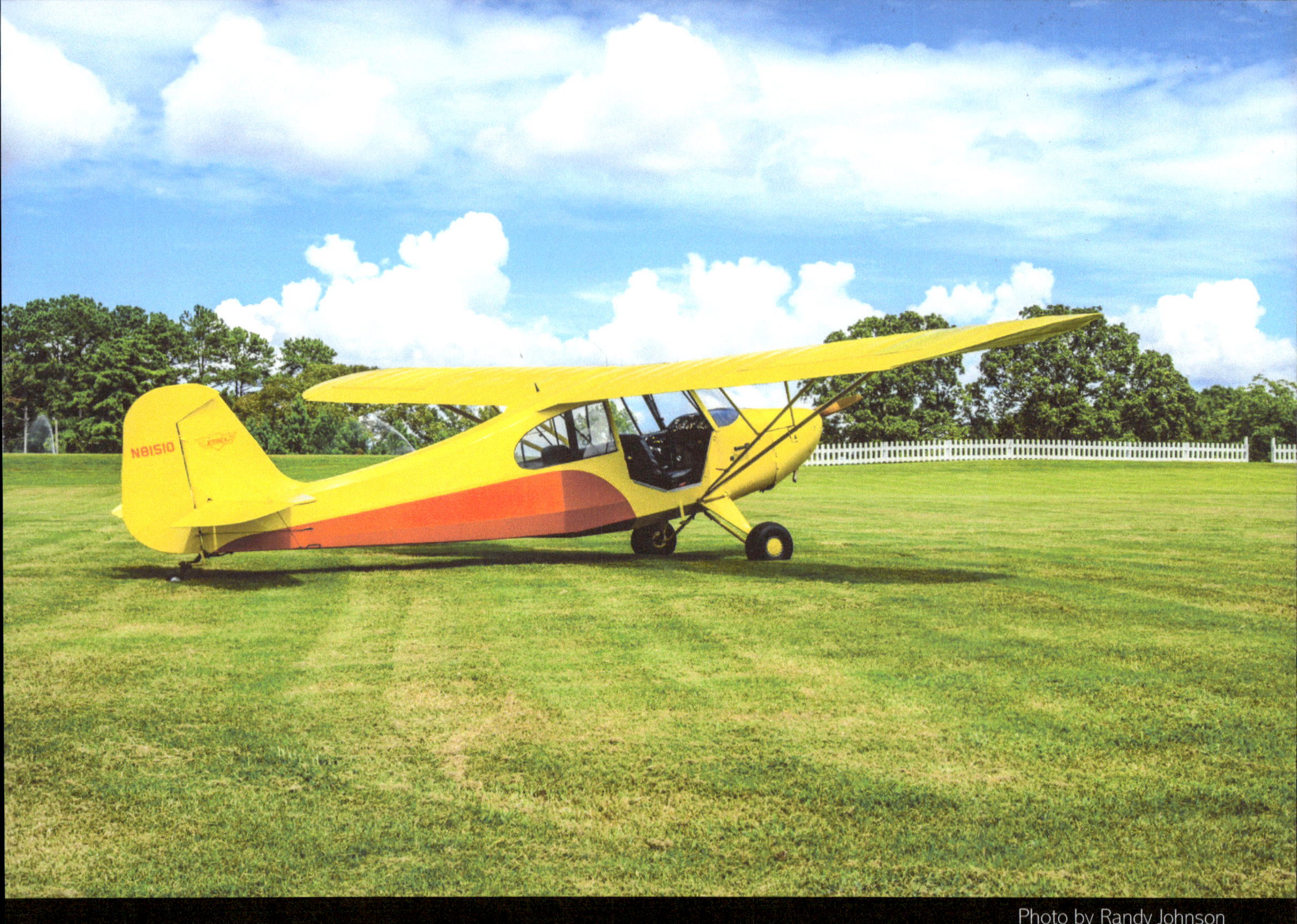

Photo by Randy Johnson

Trains

Photo by Charlene Sibaja

Trains

There is a certain air of romance when traveling by train; it evokes a sense of adventure, but somehow it remains to be a relaxed and refined method from travelling from point A to point B. A person can sit as they stare longingly out the window while the train chugs in the background, and the person can easily just glance out the window and see the wonders the world has to bring.

Richard Trevithick is an example that people can turn out to be so much more than others expect. He died in poverty in an unmarked grave, and when he was younger he was described as slow, obstinate, lazy, and practically illiterate. Though at a glance any person might assume that he was just an unimportant blip in history, but Trevithick had a knack at solving problems that experienced engineers could not solve themselves, because of this he obtained his first job as an engineer at the age of 19.

The steam engine used at this time was the one created by James Watt, which had a major impact in the Industrial Revolution. Though the engine was a marvel of technology, it was not optimal for use as a locomotive; it was too massive, and the pressure was purposely low in fear of the strong steam being too dangerous to harness. Trevithick disagreed and built a working model harnessing high pressure steam, which led to him being the first to successfully harness high pressure steam to create the first steam railway locomotive in 1803. As years went on he perfected his engine, and one powered the world's first dredgers in 1806. Trevithick went on and made history in the field of engineering, perfecting these engines, but ultimately was forgotten as other engineers profited from his inventions. He was overshadowed by other inventors such as George Stephenson, who is the named the principal inventor of the railroad locomotive.

Thanks to people who advanced in the engineering of the locomotive, we have been enjoying trains for centuries. The popularity of trains even permeated into pop culture. From movies such as Alfred Hitchcock's *North by Northwest*, audience could see what the luxury trains had to offer on trains such as "The Most Famous Train in the World." Hitchcock's narrative also gave trains the image of mystery and untold adventure. Though this train, the 20th Century Limited, was discontinued you can have a similar experience on the 49 Lake Shore Limited that travels between New York and Chicago, just like the movie.

Trains also found their way into other media such as songs like Journey's popular "Don't Stop Believin'," books such as *Murder on the Orient Express*, and even in the art of famous painters like Van Gogh and Monet. Since trains was one of the earliest ways to travel somewhat comfortably long distances, they are associated with adventure and promise. This encapsulates the romantic feeling and nostalgia trains have even today.

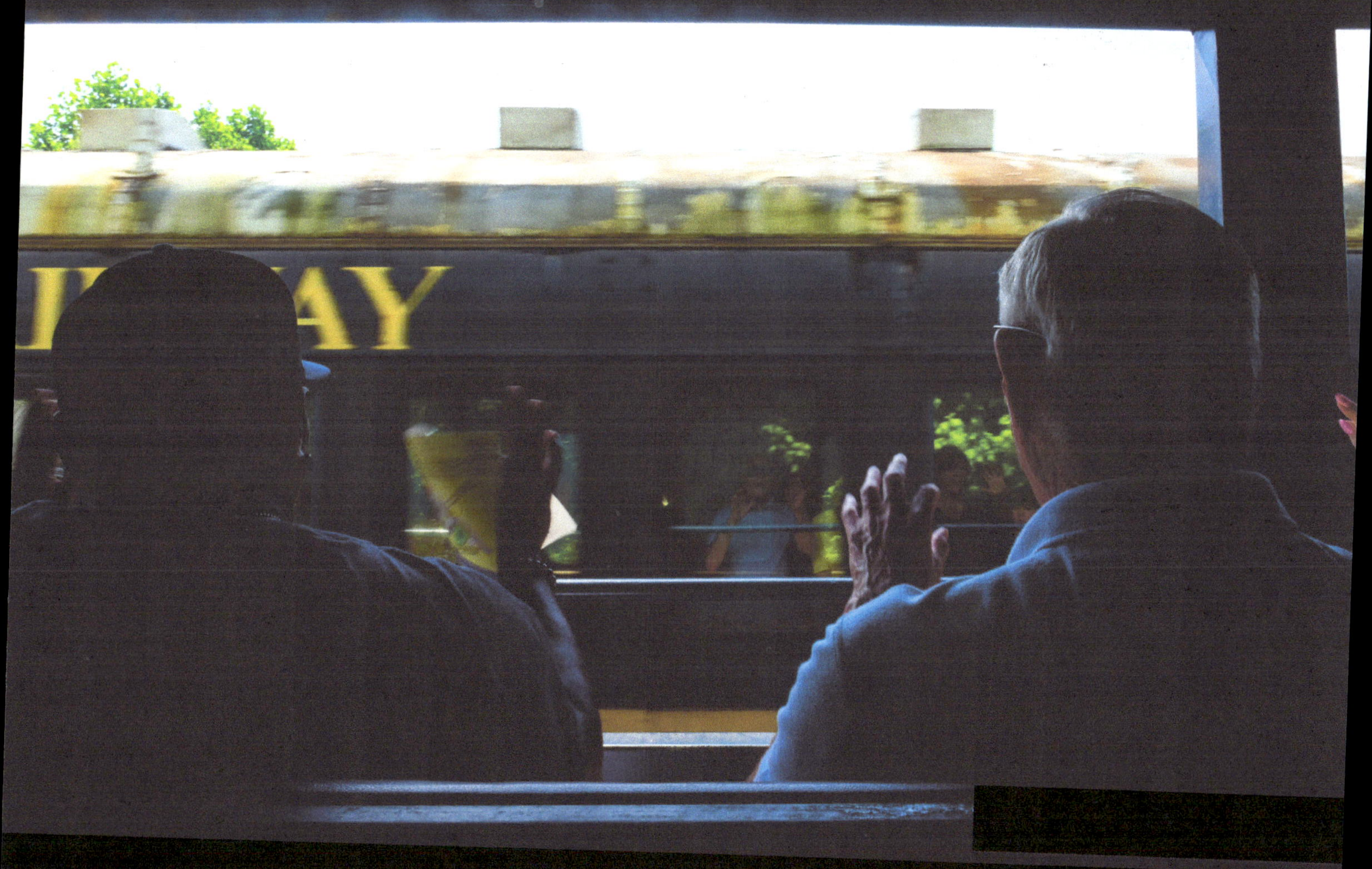

Photo Charlene Sibaja

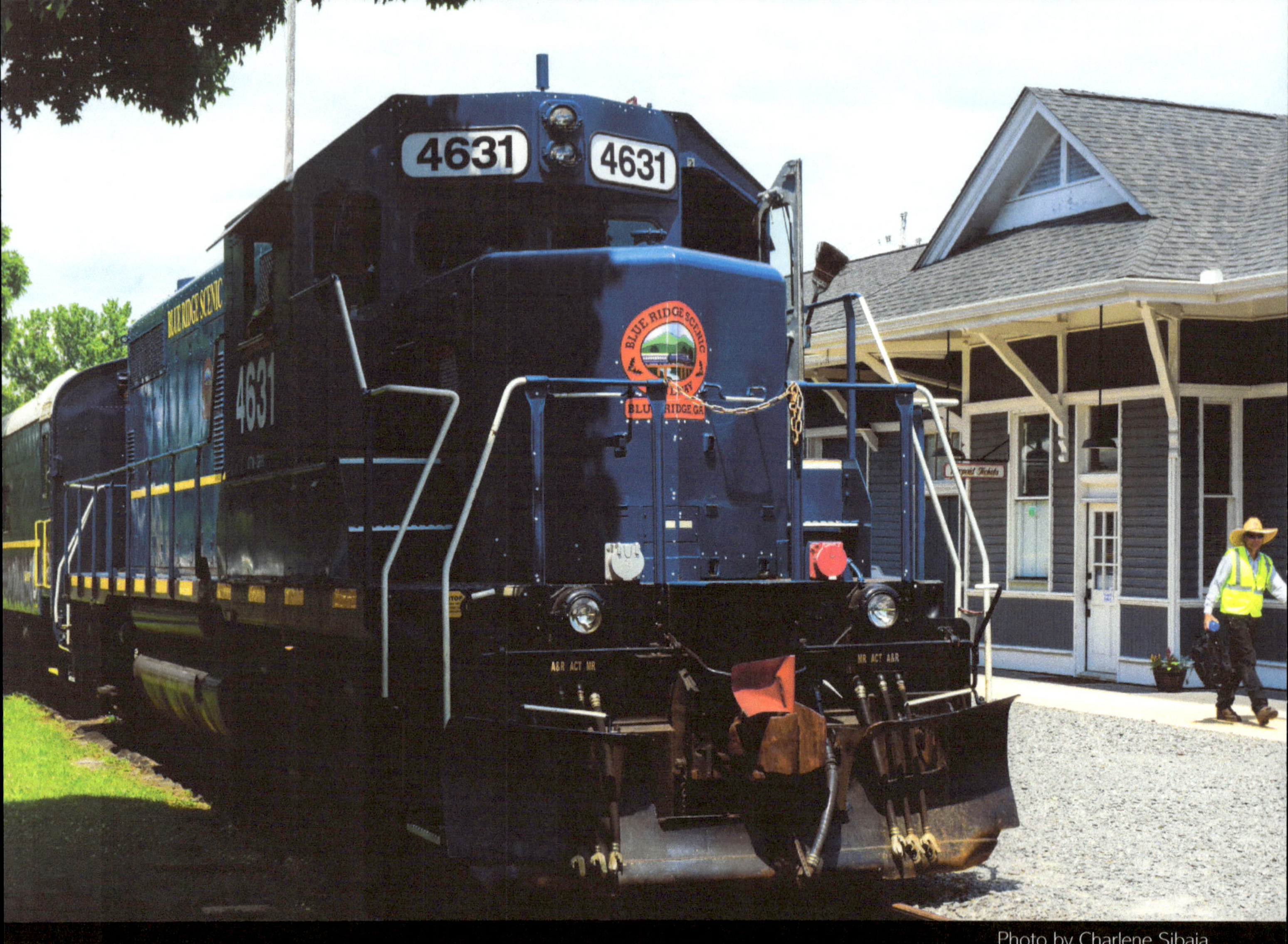

Photo by Charlene Sibaja

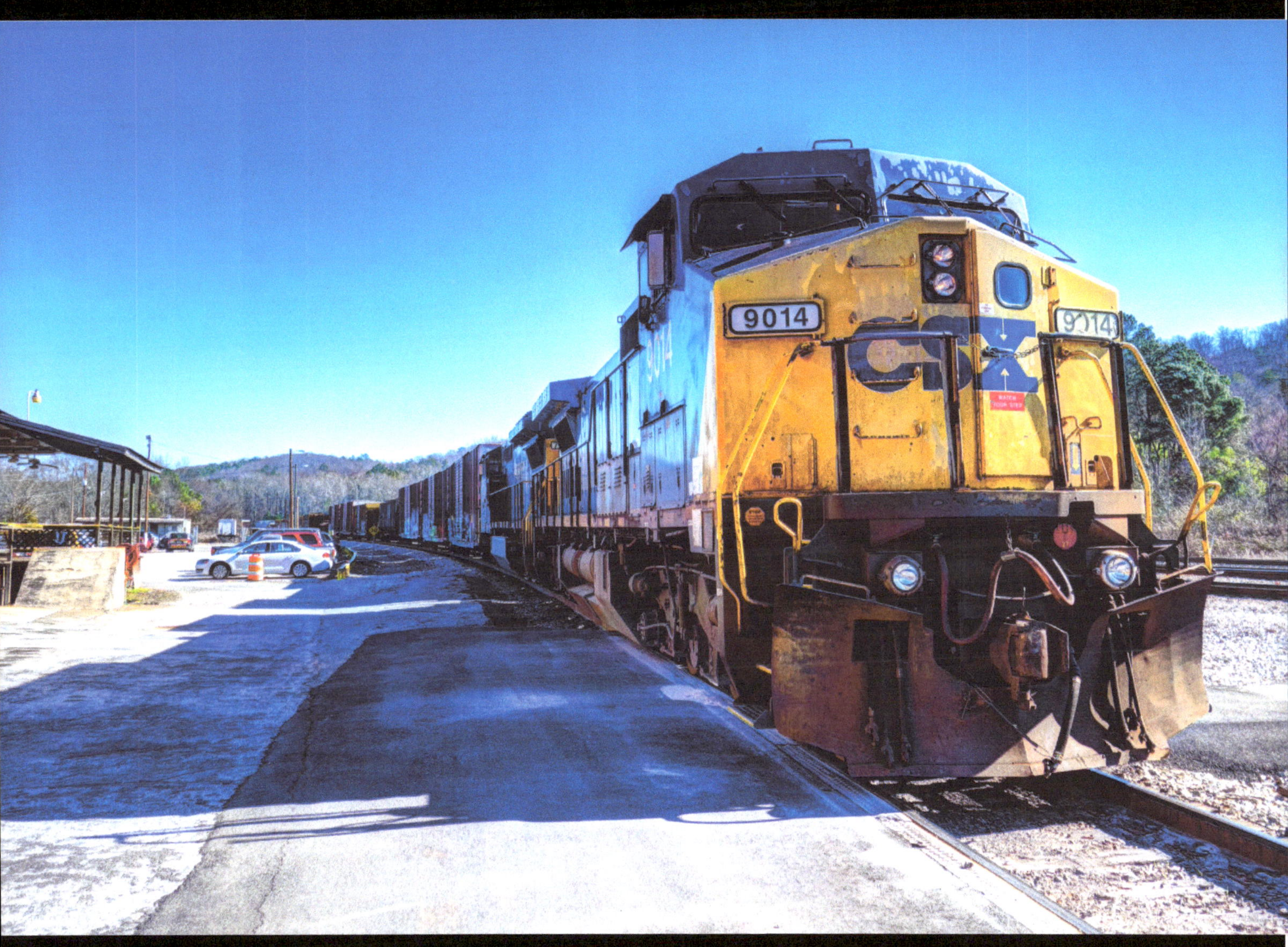

Photo by Jeff Clough

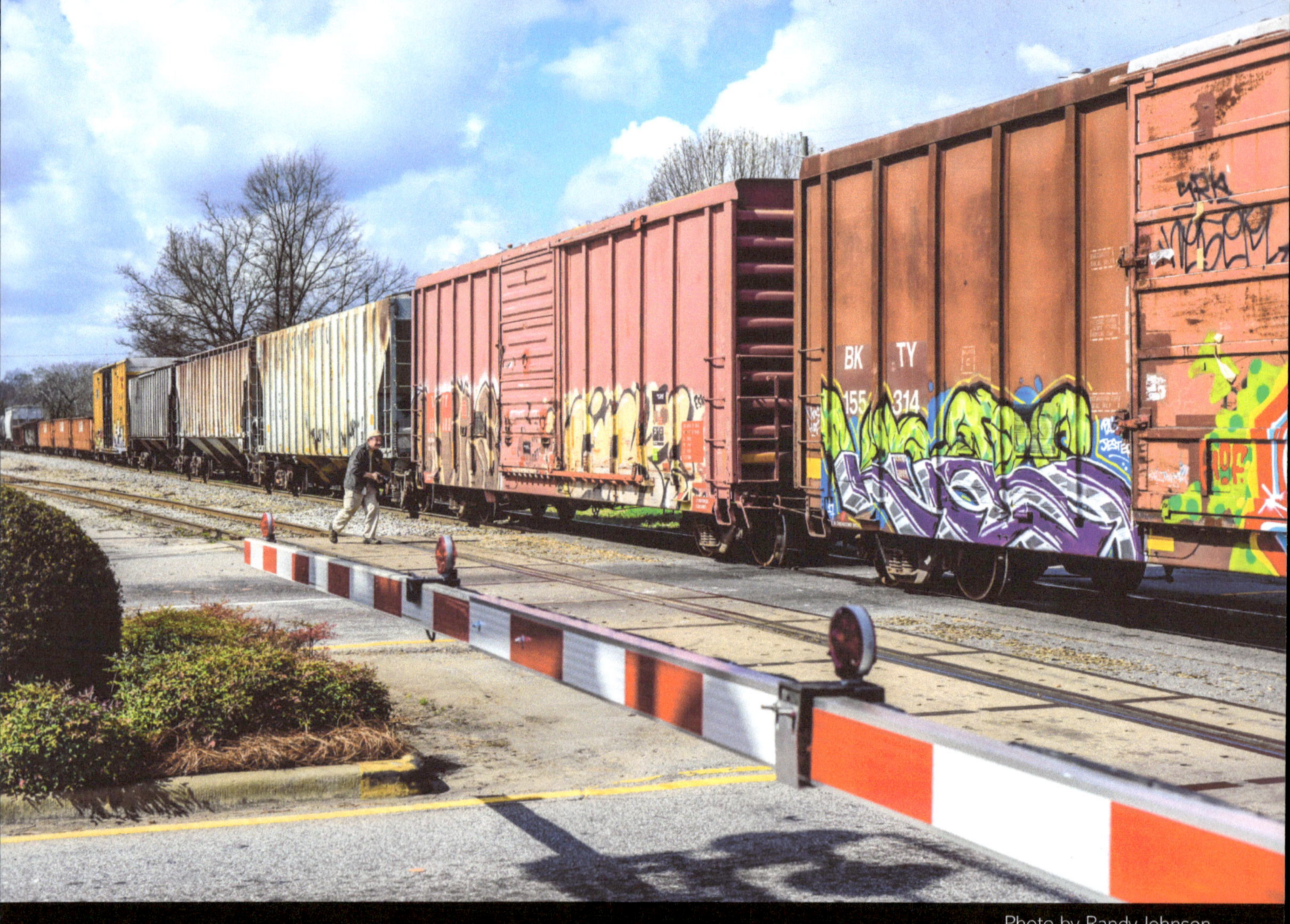

Photo by Randy Johnson

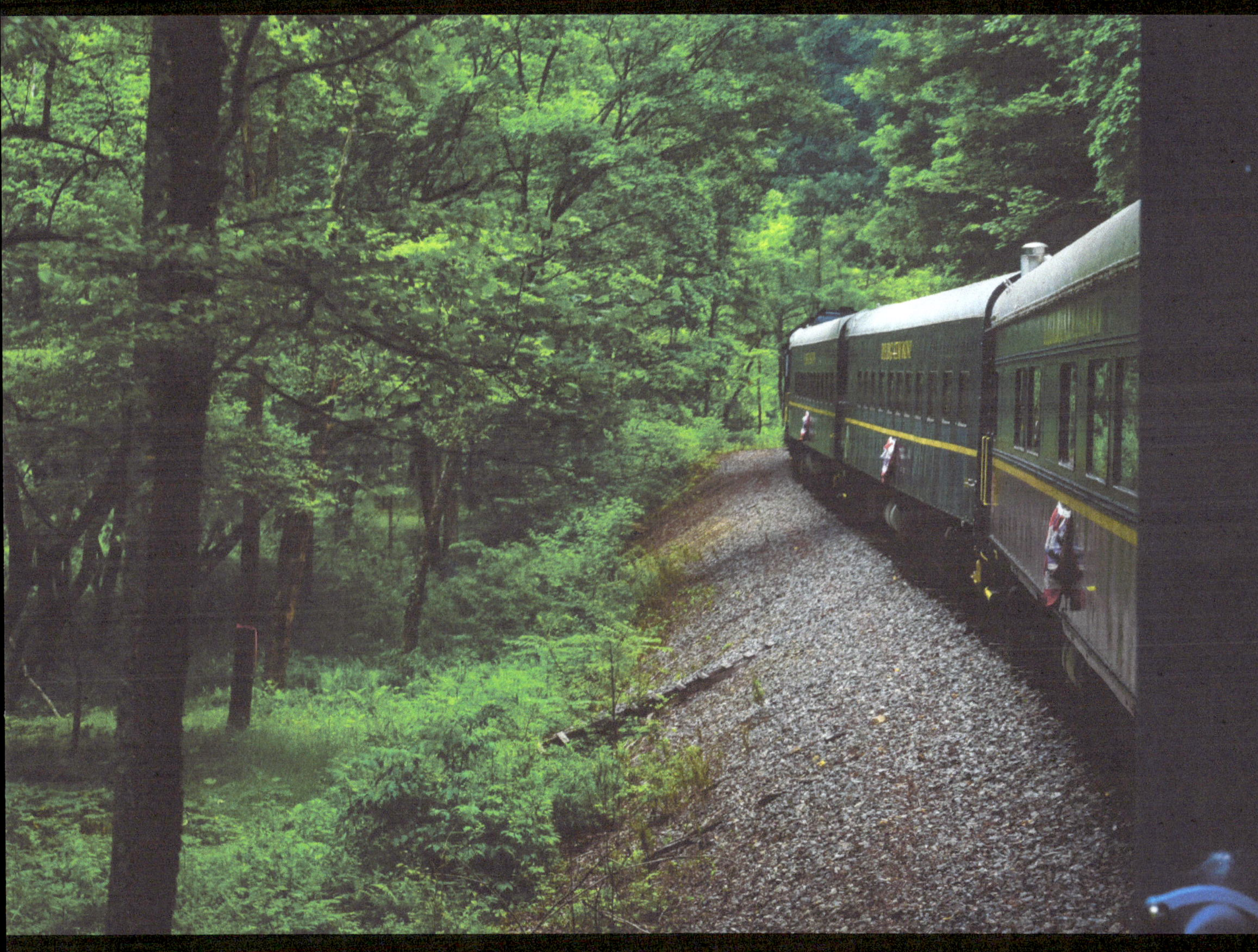

Photo by Roger Sibaja

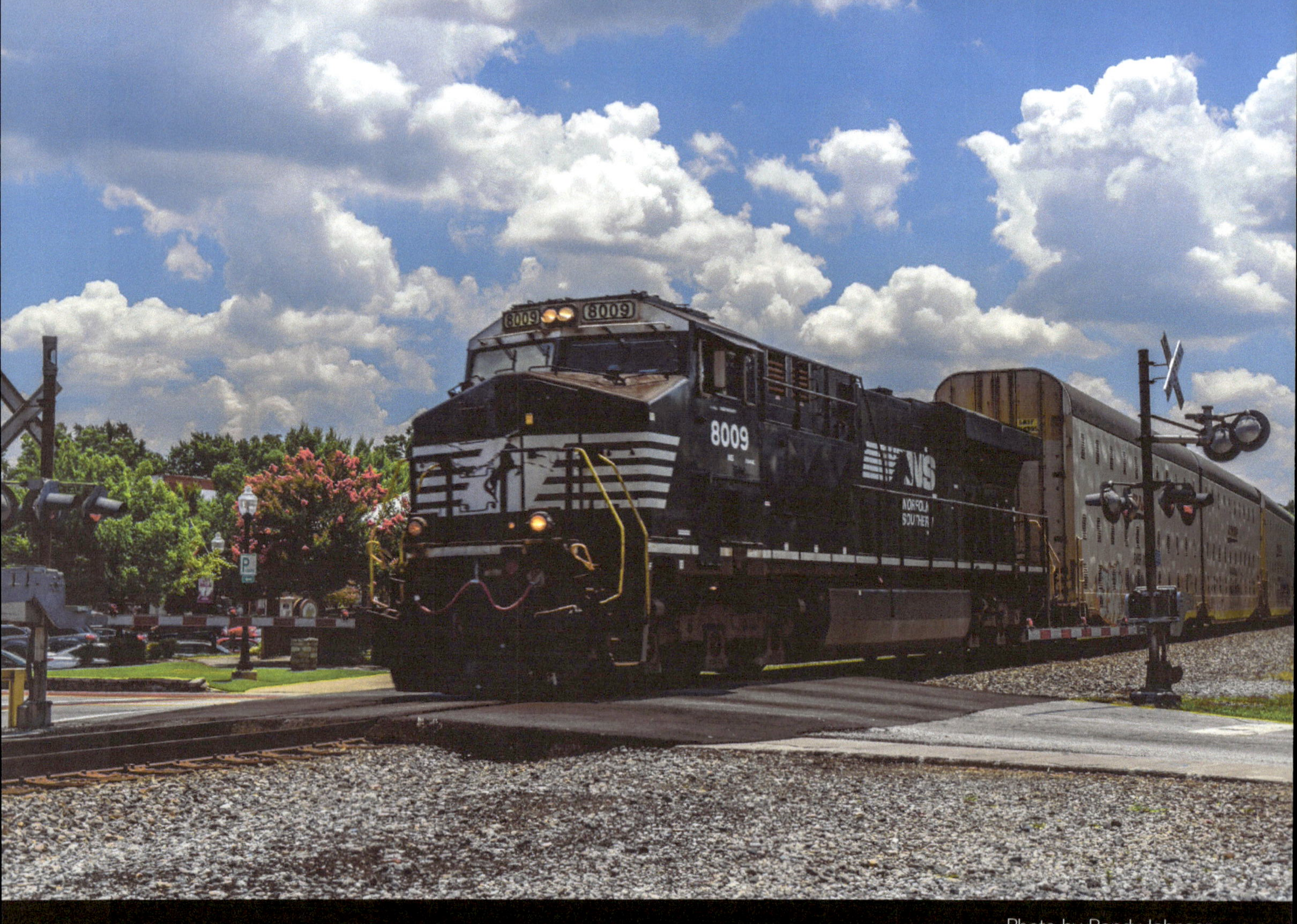

Photo by Randy Johnson

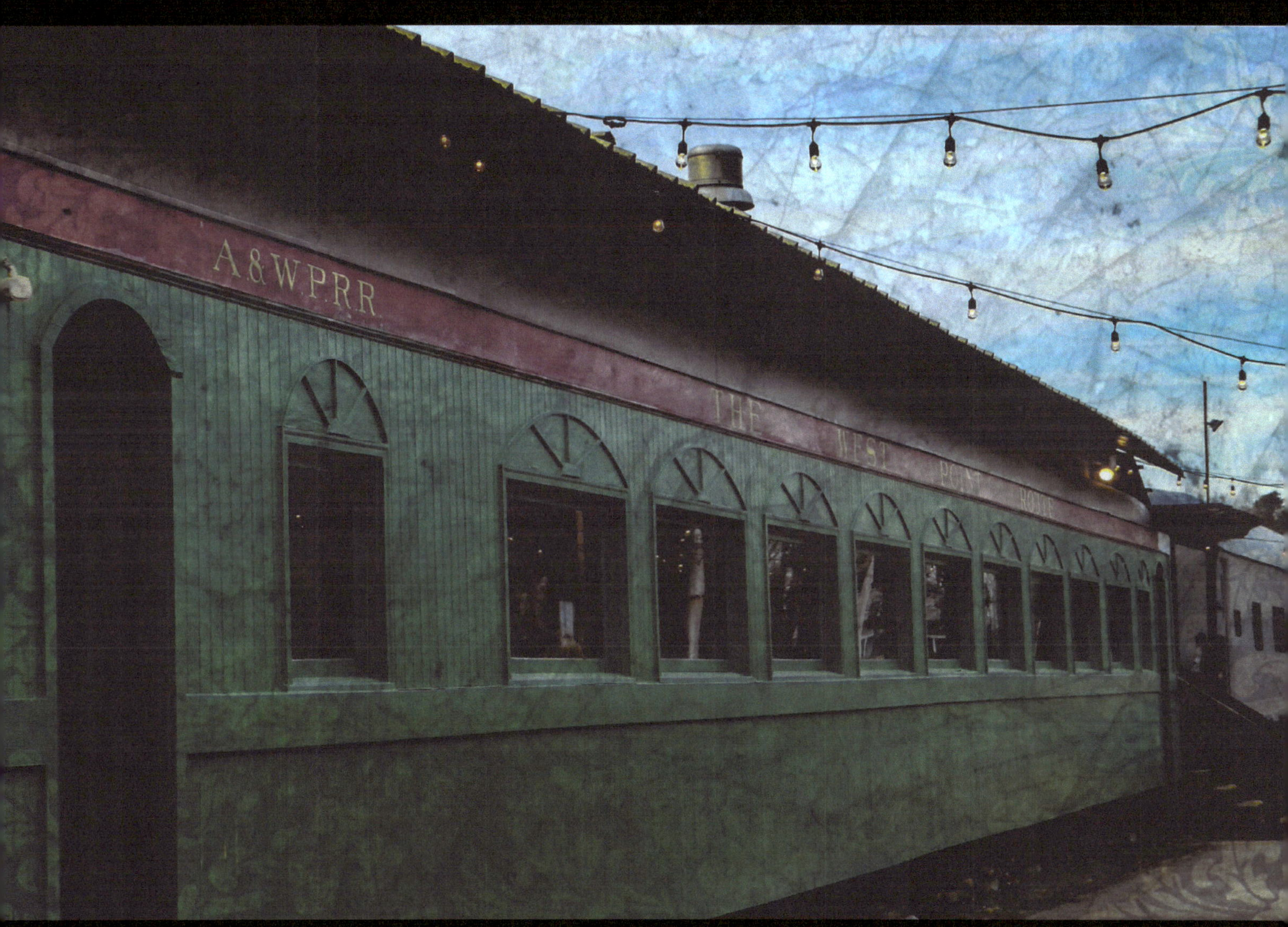

Photo by Lynn Murphy

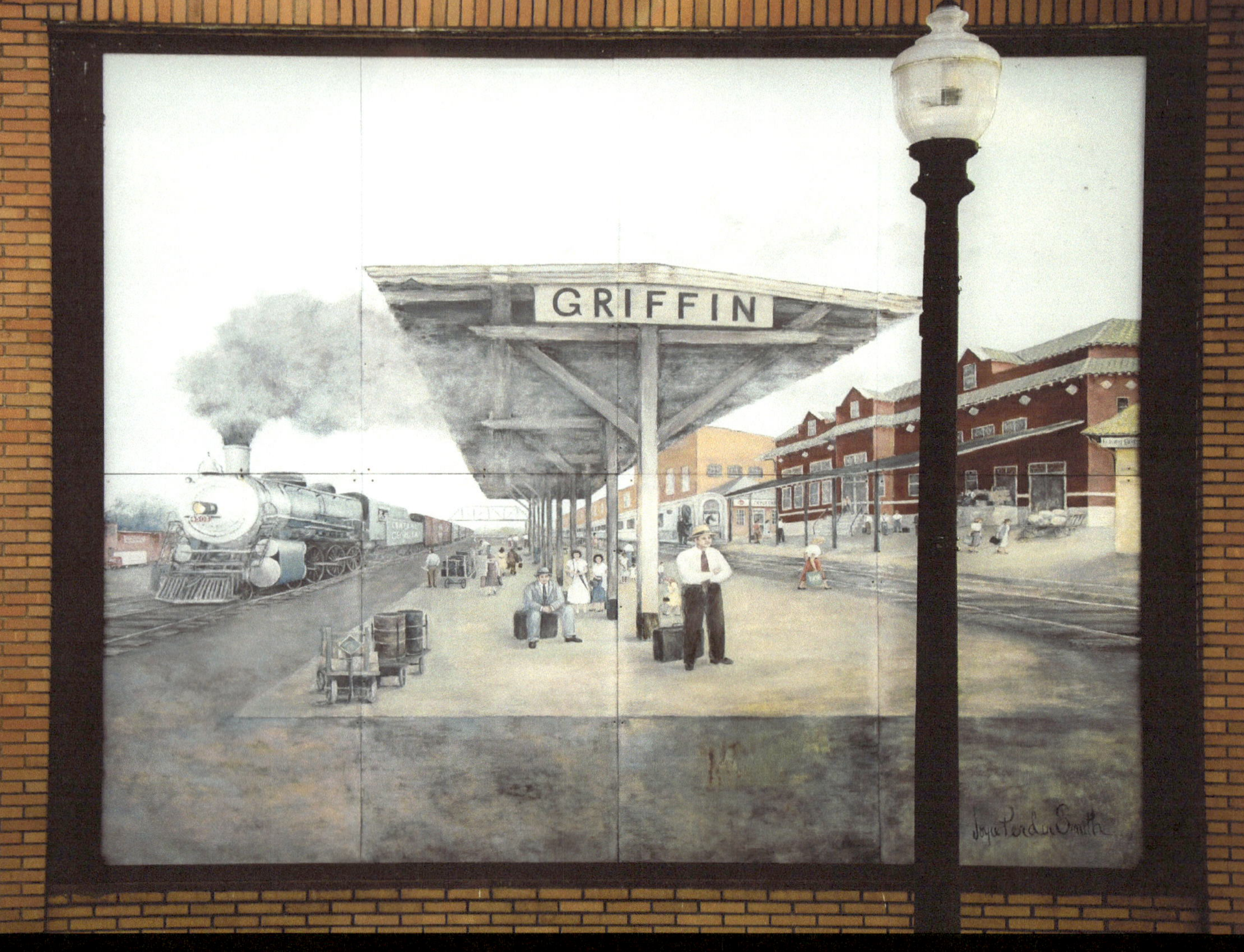

Photo by Jim Johns

Automobiles

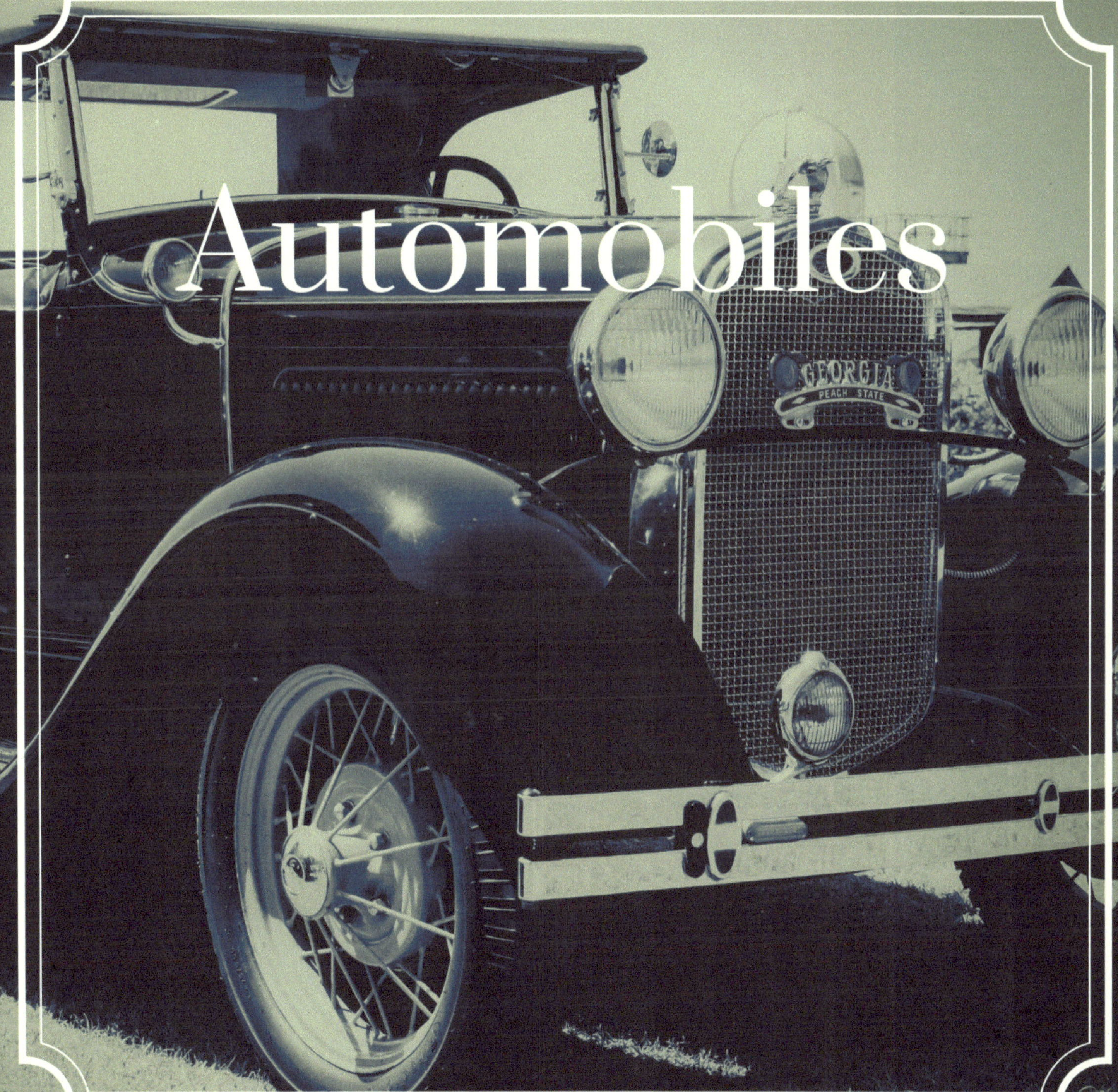

Photo by Charlene Sibaja

Automobiles

Before the car, people used carriages to travel long distances. If a person did not have a carriage, they could ride a bike or walk. Transportation would be slow and came with complications, such as taking care of the horse or worrying about fatigue. Many people began yearning for a way to travel quicker and more conveniently. This began the spark to find a solution.

Today we have cars like the Bugatti Veyron Super Sport that can reach a speed of 267 mph and go from 0 to 60 in 2.4 seconds. It would be a travesty to write a book about accelerating without discussing automobiles. Since the beginning of time, man has wanted to go faster and longer while conserving energy, with cars we got a step closer.

Roger Bacon (1214-1292), a Franciscan Friar, predicted and wrote about how carts would move without animals at unbelievable speeds. He also envisioned that someday man would have airplanes, submarines, steamships, and scuba gear. Homer and Leonardo da Vinci both also foresaw the revolutionary invention of the automobile.

Bacon, Homer, and da Vinci inspired countless others to experiment on the quest to find the holy grail of the automobile. There have been many types of automobiles - steam, electric, and gas. Karl Benz, a German engineer, designed the world's first practical automobile that was powered by an internal combustion engine.

Even though Karl Benz passed away a long time ago, his name lives on in his company Mercedes-Benz. The cars they sell today are known for their reliability and are usually found in the lists by business magazines as one of the most reliable cars on the market.

Today we have several different options when it comes to choosing a vehicle. Do you want to travel to the country? Maybe you should buy an RV. Want a car that can maneuver quickly as you feel the wind on your skin? A convertible might be more your speed. The simple creation of the car was not enough. Car manufacturers realized that every person is different, and they deserve an automobile that could keep up.

One of the deviations was the truck. They needed more horsepower and space in order to carry materials. They act as the workhorses of a nation, used to haul supplies or people to destinations supporting our economy or to simply bring happiness by connecting people.

Americans love their cars. We write songs about them, give them names, and make movies about them. Most of us have very fond memories of road trips, vacations, and adventures, with a car at the center. Most of us have those cars we really disliked, cars we loved and the cars we wish we had. In this section, you find cars with which people have a true connection. You might even go as far as to say these vehicles are loved.

Helpful Tip: Years ago, Henry Ford coined the phrase "tune-up" as a process to help your automobile run more efficient. Today, we realized that automobile maintenance is not only to improve engine performance, but it adds to the longevity of your automobile, so if you have a car that you are hoping to become a "Classic" keep in mind that regular maintenance can increase the life of your vehicle. Giving it life for decades to share its story.

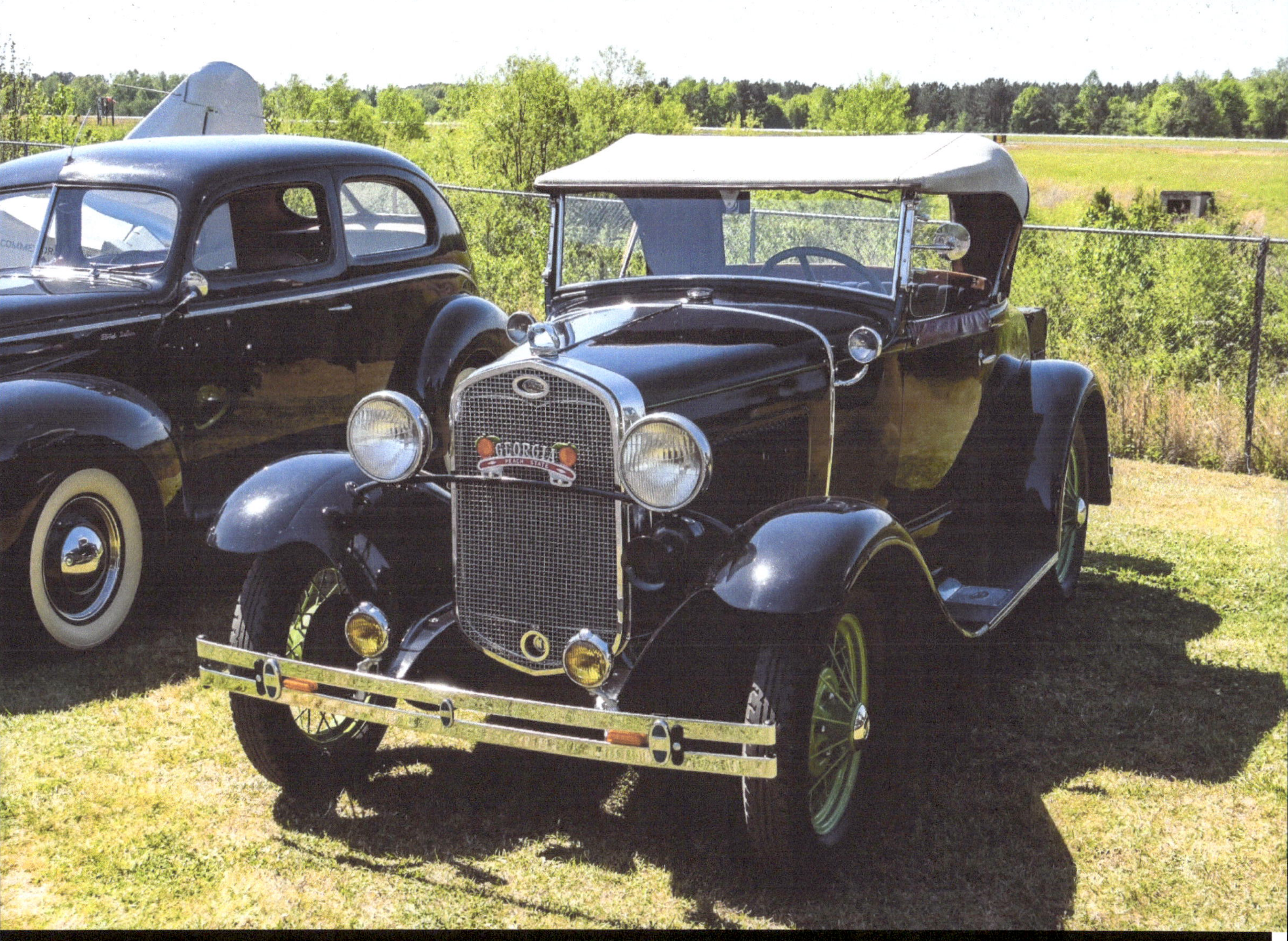

Photo Jeff Clough

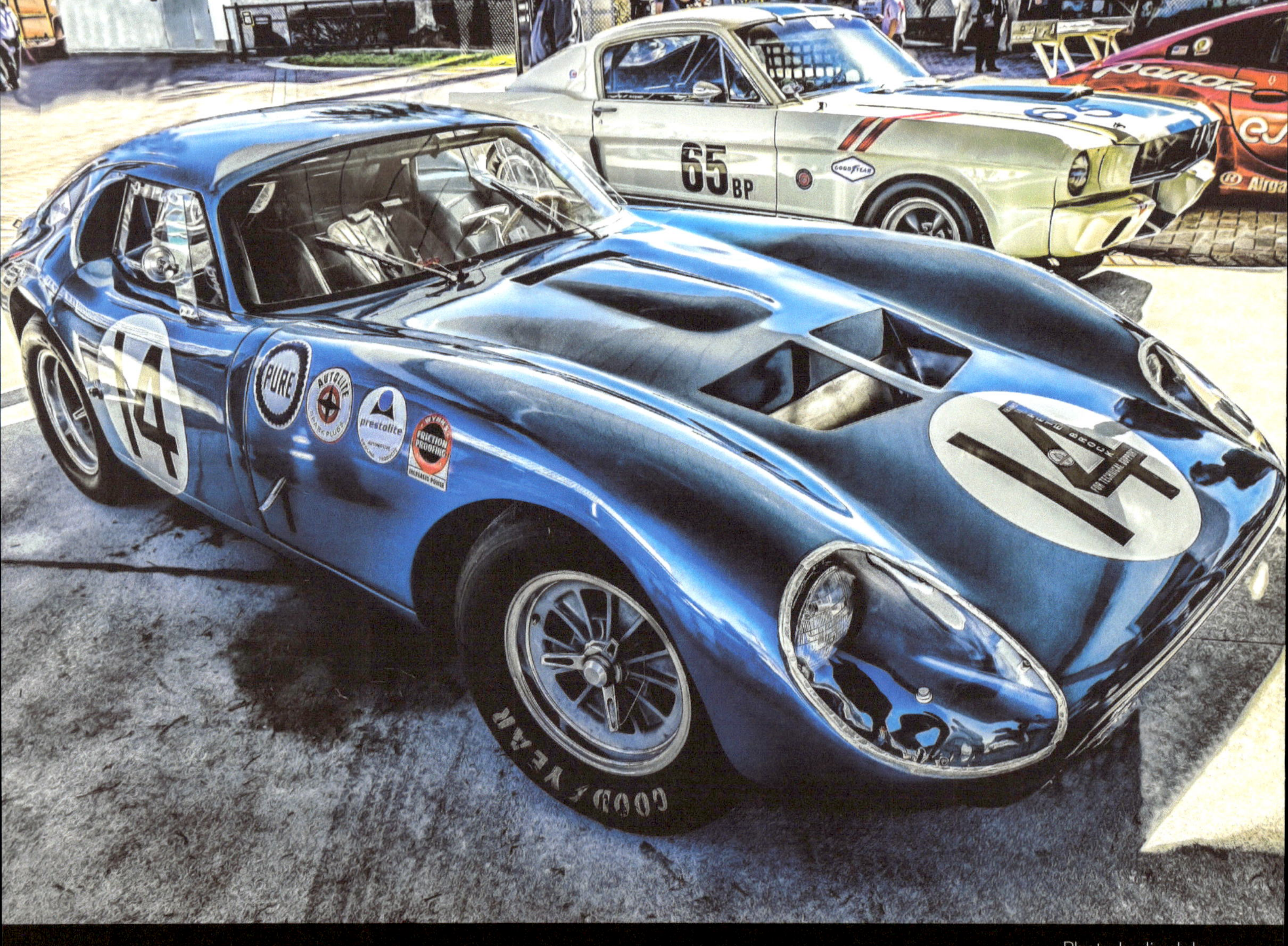

Photo by Jim Johns

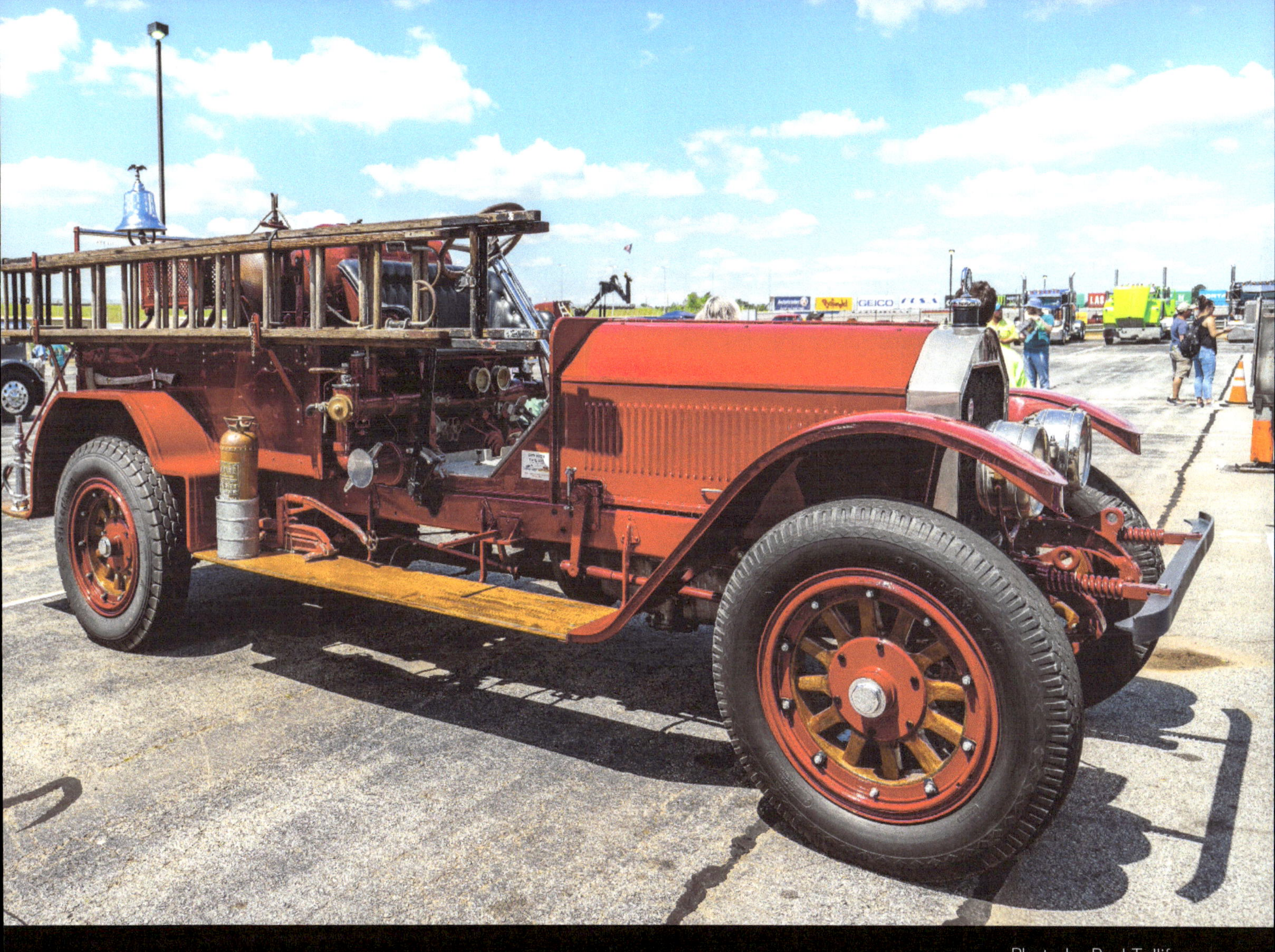

Photo by Paul Talliferro

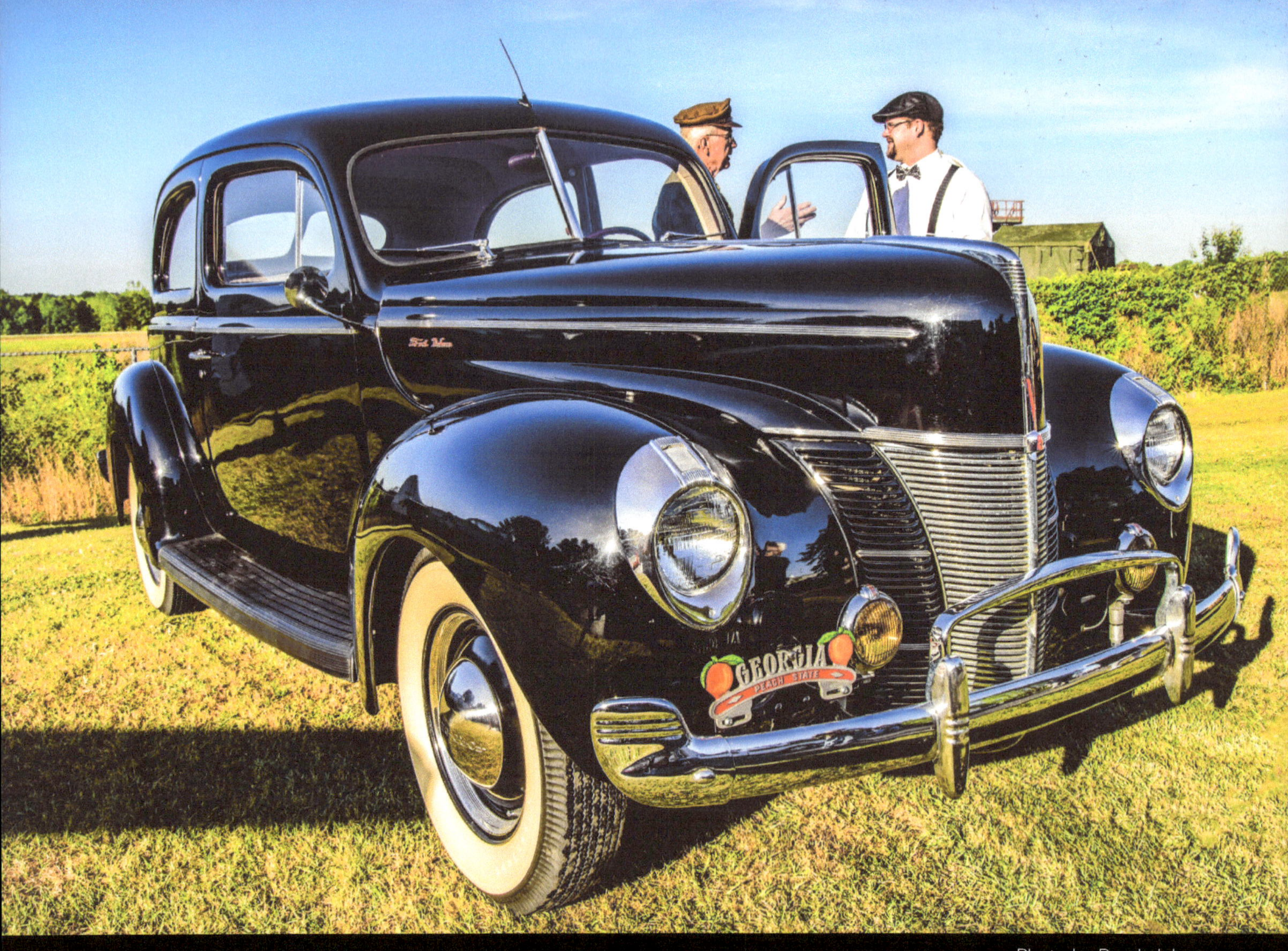

Photo by Randy Johnson

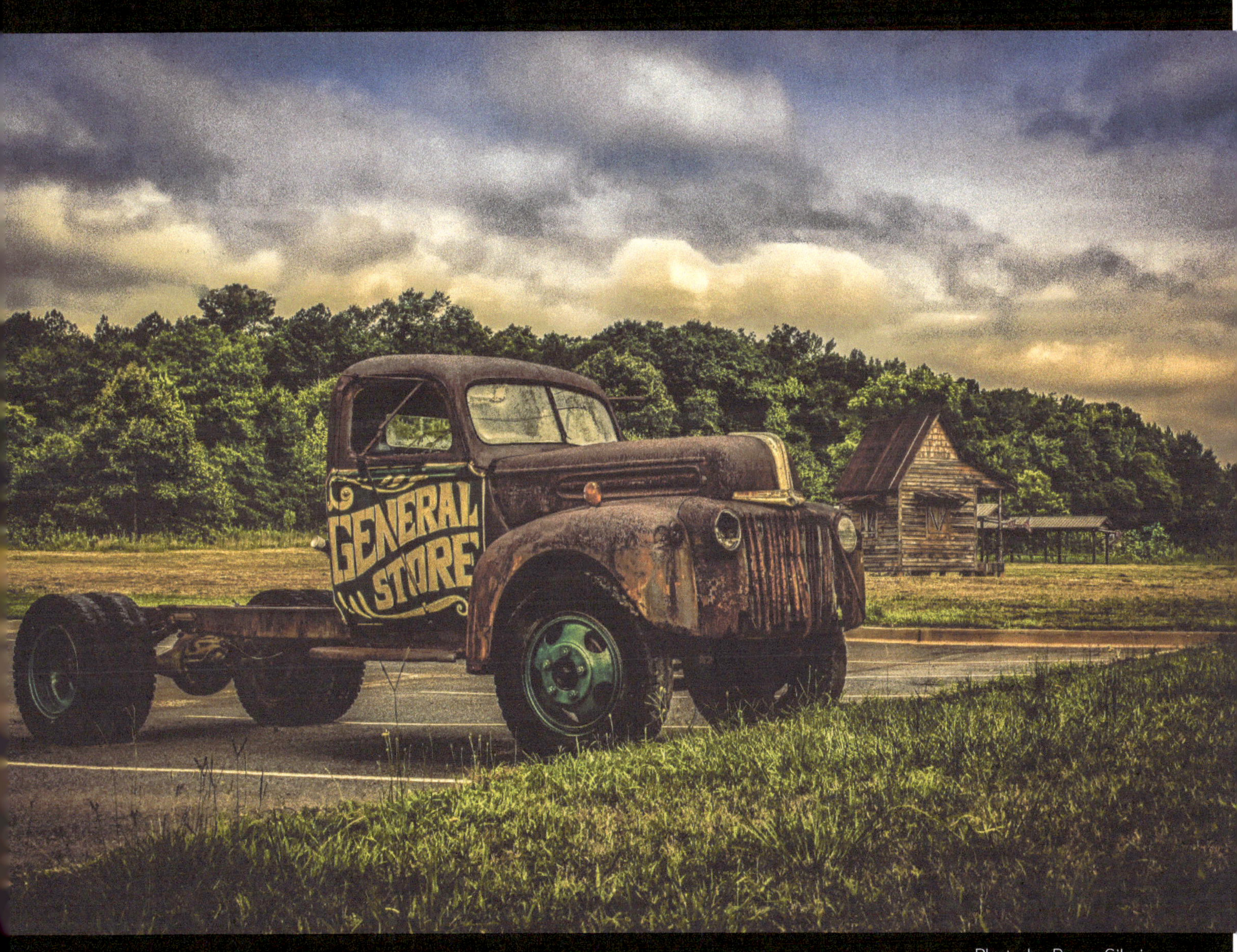

Photo by Roger Sibaja

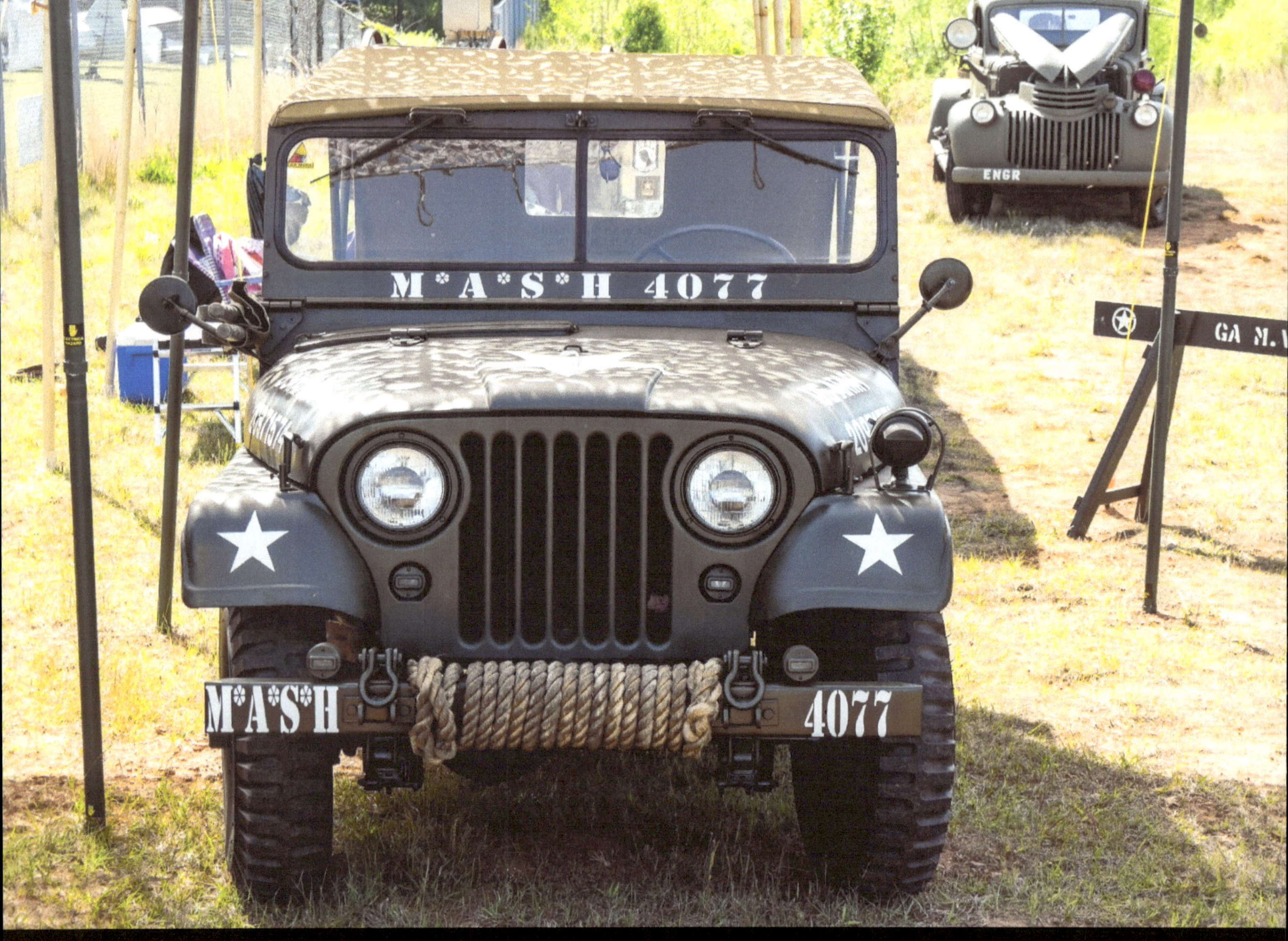

Photo by Jeff Clough

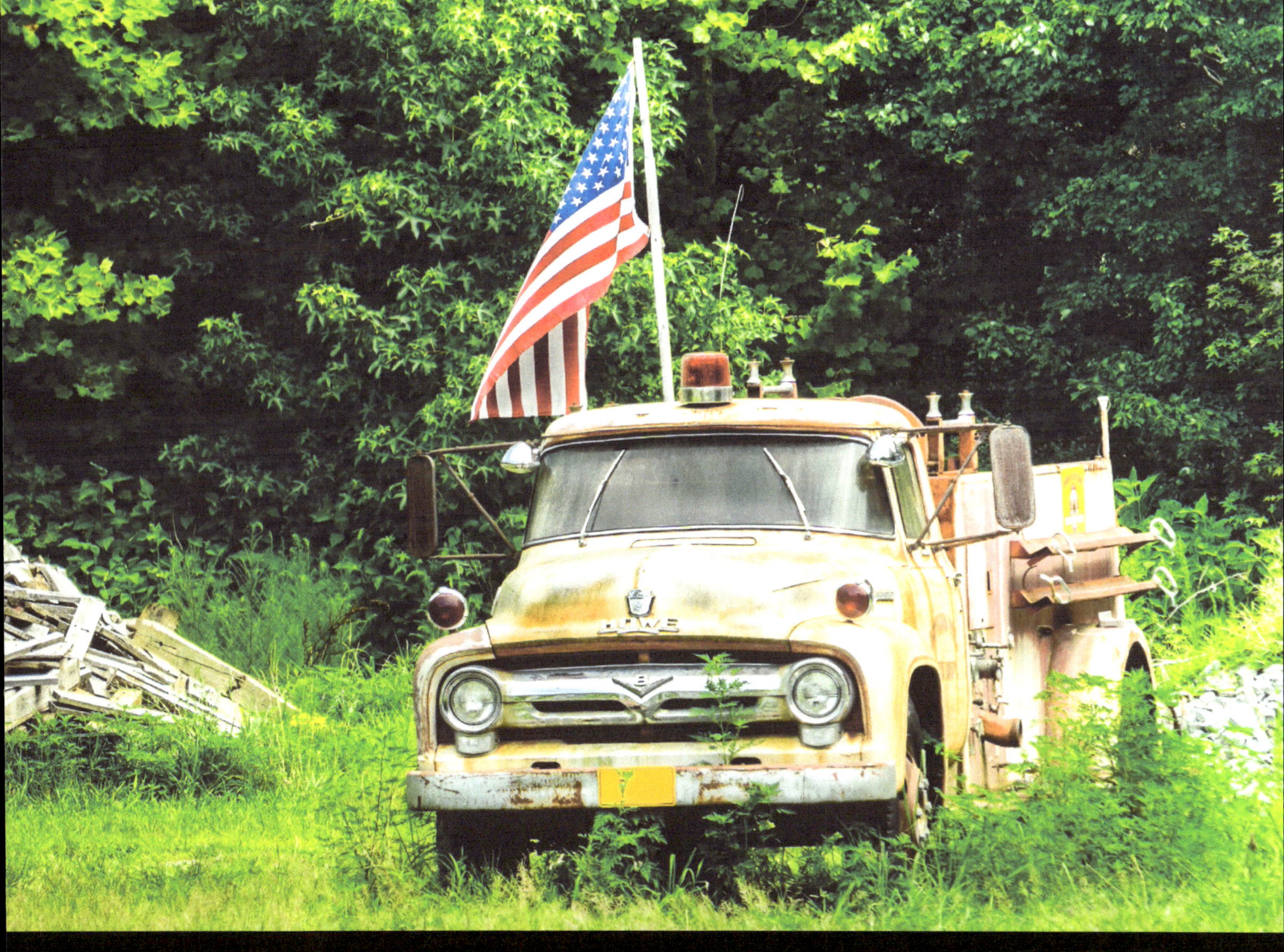

Photo by Paul Taliferro

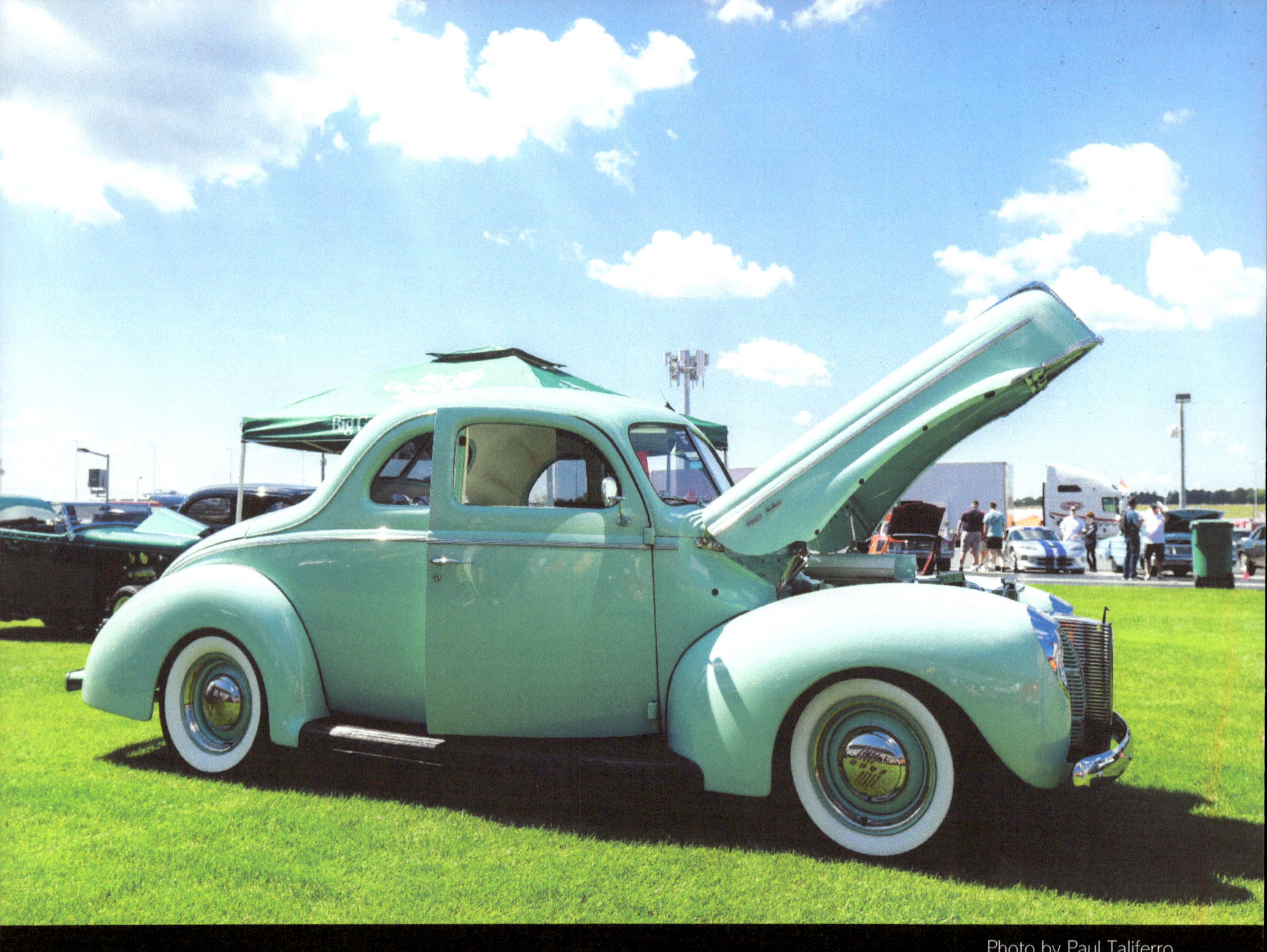

Photo by Paul Taliferro

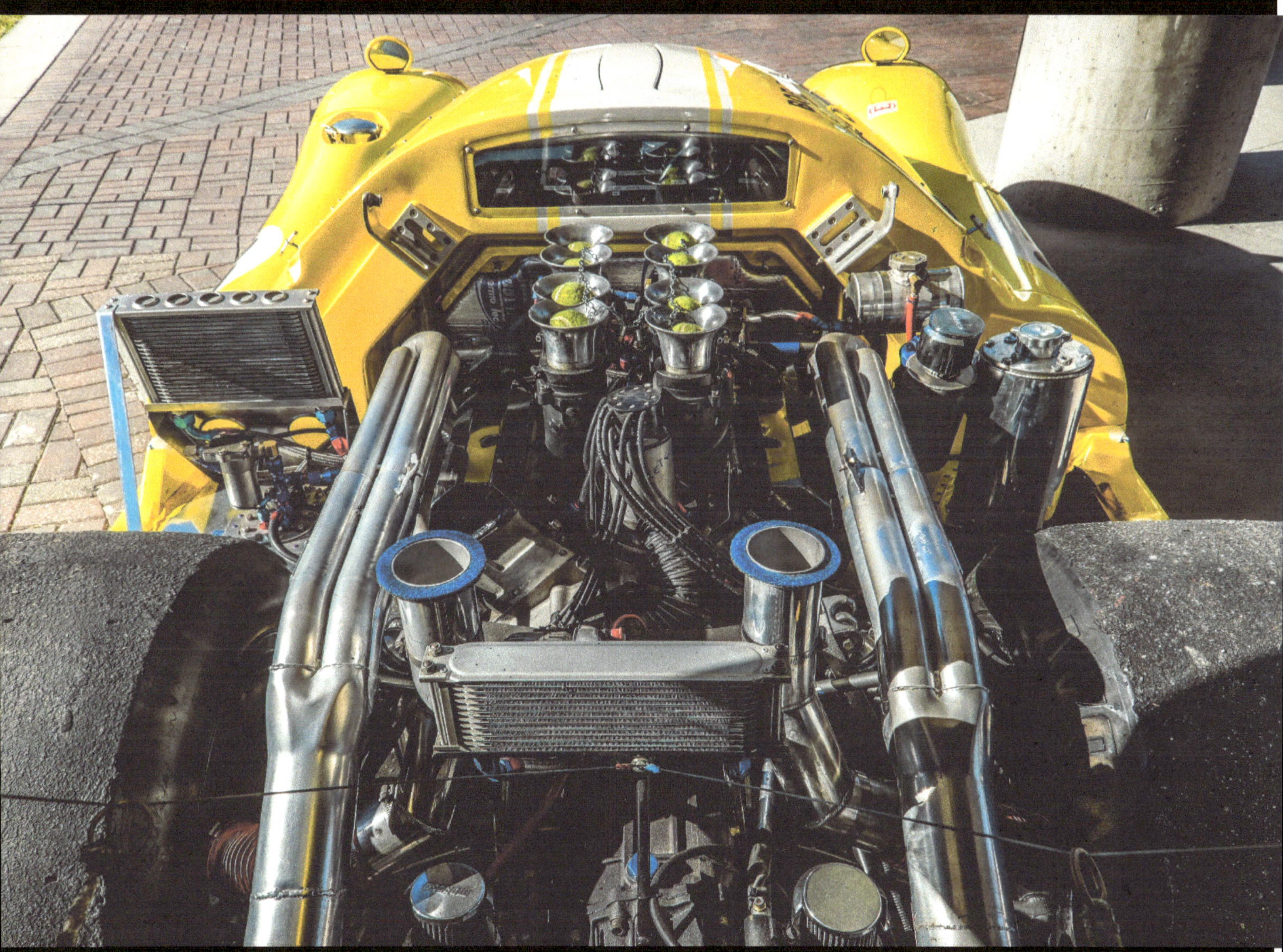

Photo by Jim Johns

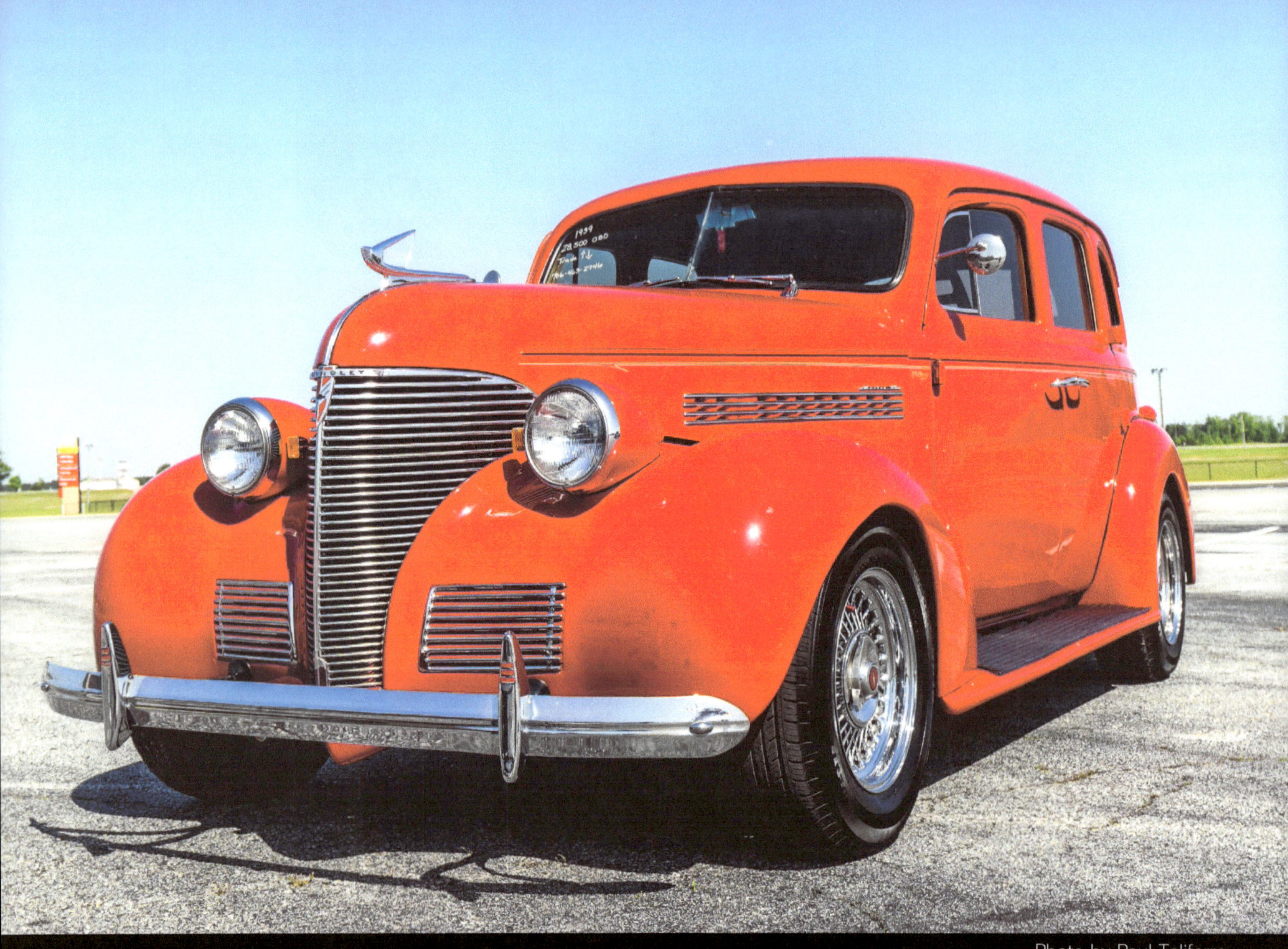

Photo by Paul Taliferro

Boats

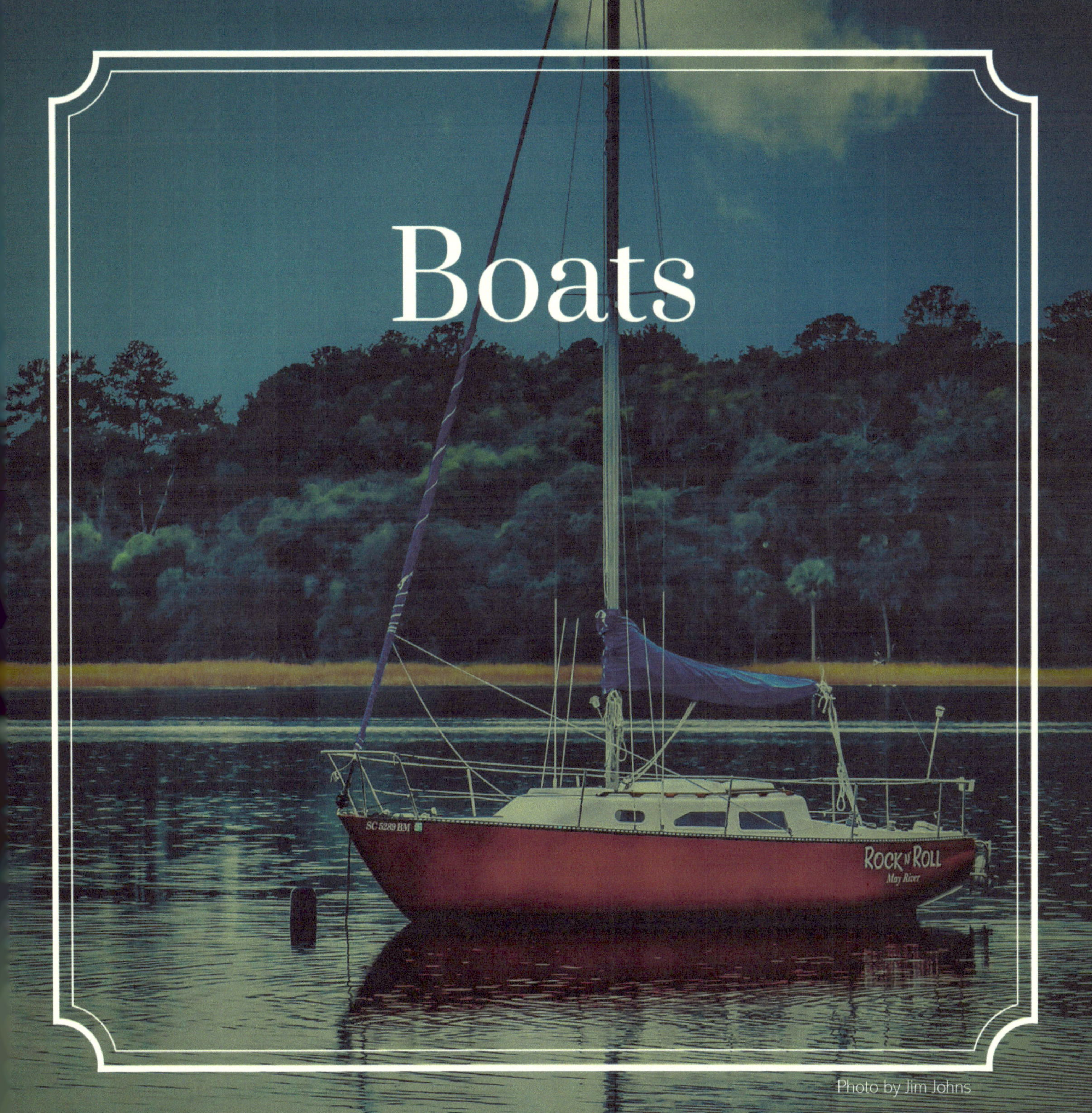

Photo by Jim Johns

Boats

Whether rafts, kayaks, canoes, or sailboats, boating is one of mankind's earliest forms of transport. Humans have used boats to explore, fish, conquer, sport, and transport goods. Luxury boats, such as cruise ships were created to be the destination itself. Cultures around the world have made their own contribution to boats, whether, for simple aesthetics or function, boats were marked by their creators.

Egyptians around 4000 BC showed the first evidence of boats. The people in Egypt relied heavily on boats because they would use the Nile to transport goods. Egyptian boats usually had a sail and oars. As the Egyptians began to venture out into the Mediterranean and the Red Seas, most boats they used were still single sailed with one level of the boat to oar.

As time progressed, it was clear that more levels were needed to assist in navigating boats. Romans began to build bireme (two-level) and trireme (three-level) boats. In the 3rd millennium BC, the Egyptians began to travel to Crete and Phoenicia.

The Cretan and Phoenician took notice of the ship and created ships that specialized for trading. The design of these ships also was used for the basic functions for cargo ships and warships. Warships had to be able to maneuver quickly and be spacious to hold the troops. Trading ships focused on tonnage and with as little crew as possible.

Trading ships also needed to be taller, because people realized that some seas' higher waves would swamp the oarsman. They began creating taller ships, but the long oars were unreliable. This prompted people to recognize the necessity of specializing the ships, and ship designing became an important job of that time.

As time continued people all around the world created their own types of ships: the Vikings built longboats to sail the open sea, the Chinese had boats called junks that used a rudder to steer, and eventually in America in 1787 John Fitch made a successful trial of a steamboat.

Though at this time steamboats were just in experimental stages, Robert Fulton found a way to turn them from an experiment to a commercial success. From then on people just continued improving the boats. Giving boats functions and specializing more and more. From fishing boats to speedboats, people have found new ways to use boats as a vehicle.

Steamships became a fascination of people. Luxury boats were created for the people who began to flock to boats to see foreign lands or just to stare out in the water. One of the most famous examples of this was the British luxury steamship, The Titanic. A vessel knew today because of the tragedy and success of the movie based upon the event of the ship.

Another popular film that centered on a boat, was the short film *Steamboat Willie*, 1929. This was the first Mickey Mouse film released, and it was the first time that a cartoon was synchronized with sound. The film was such a success that most people around the world know both the names of Mickey Mouse and Walt Disney.

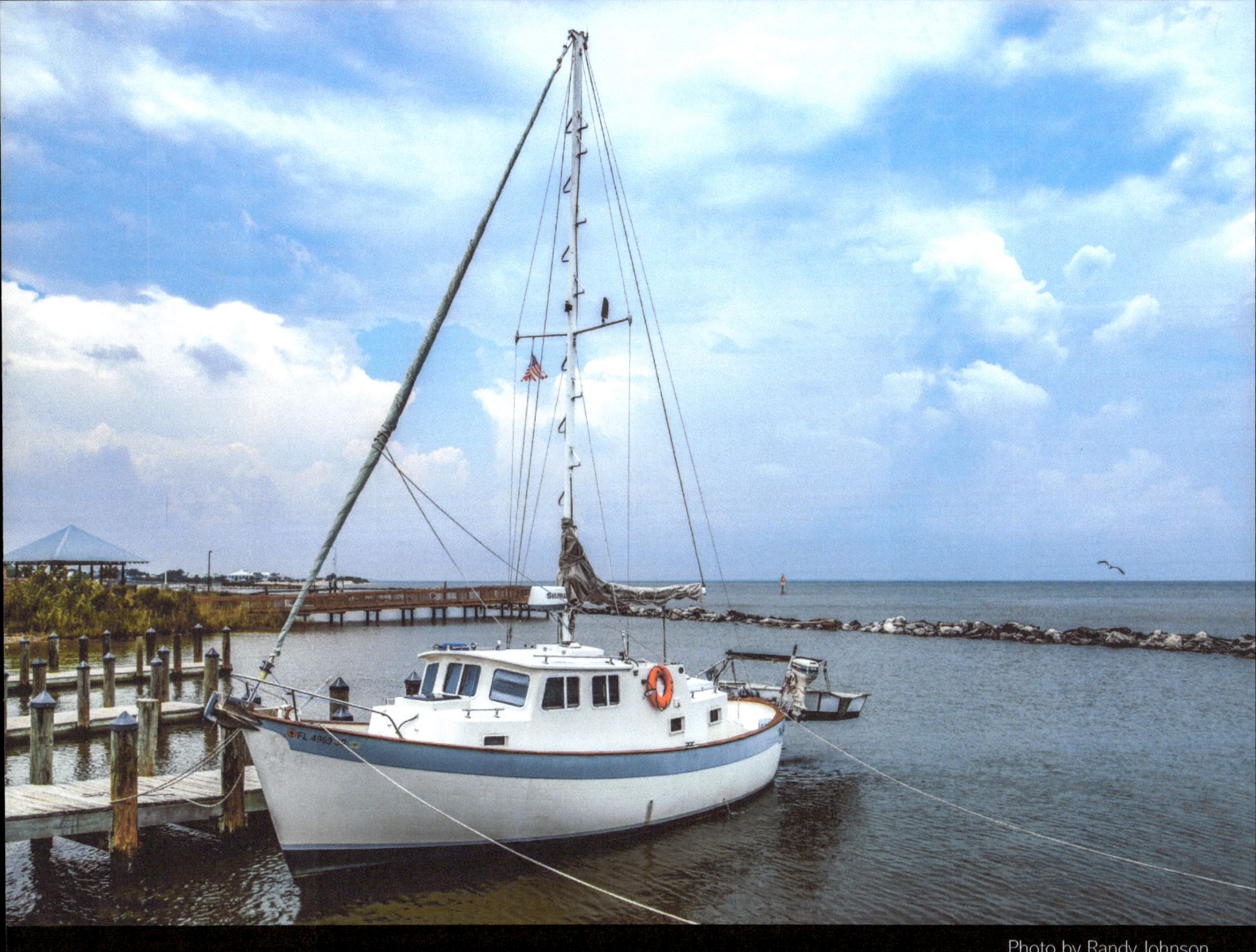

Photo by Randy Johnson

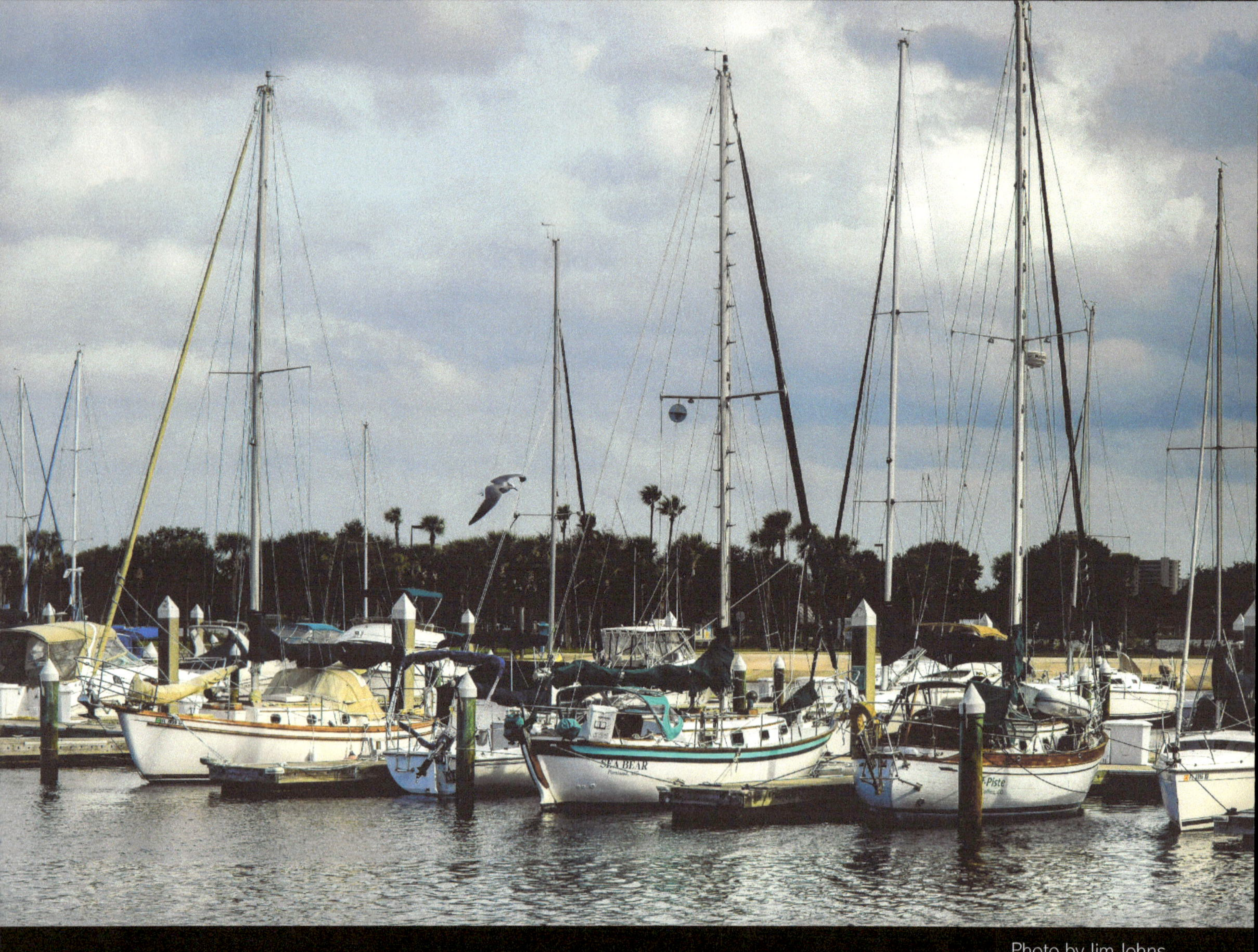

Photo by Jim Johns

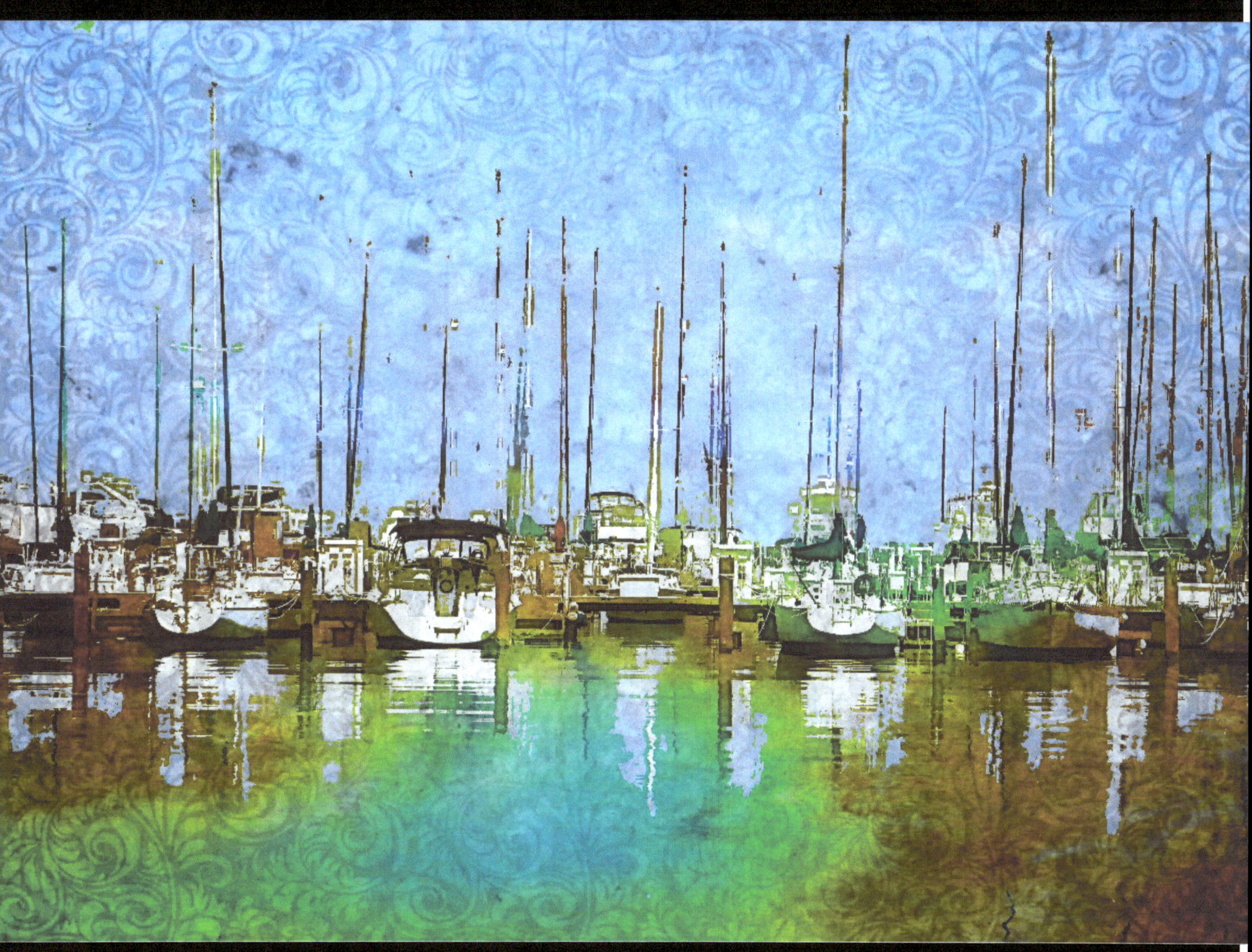

Photo by Lynn Murphy

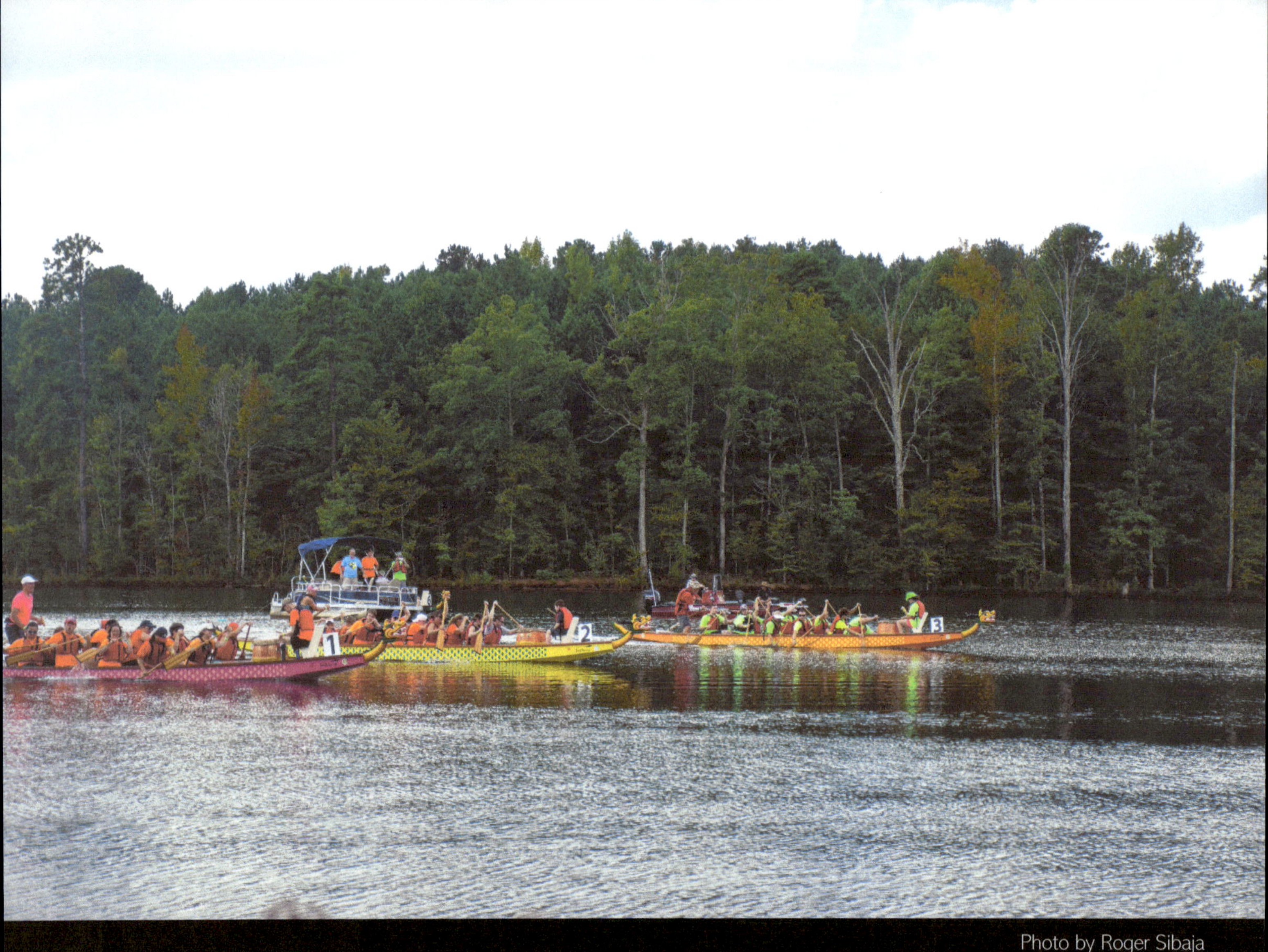

Photo by Roger Sibaja

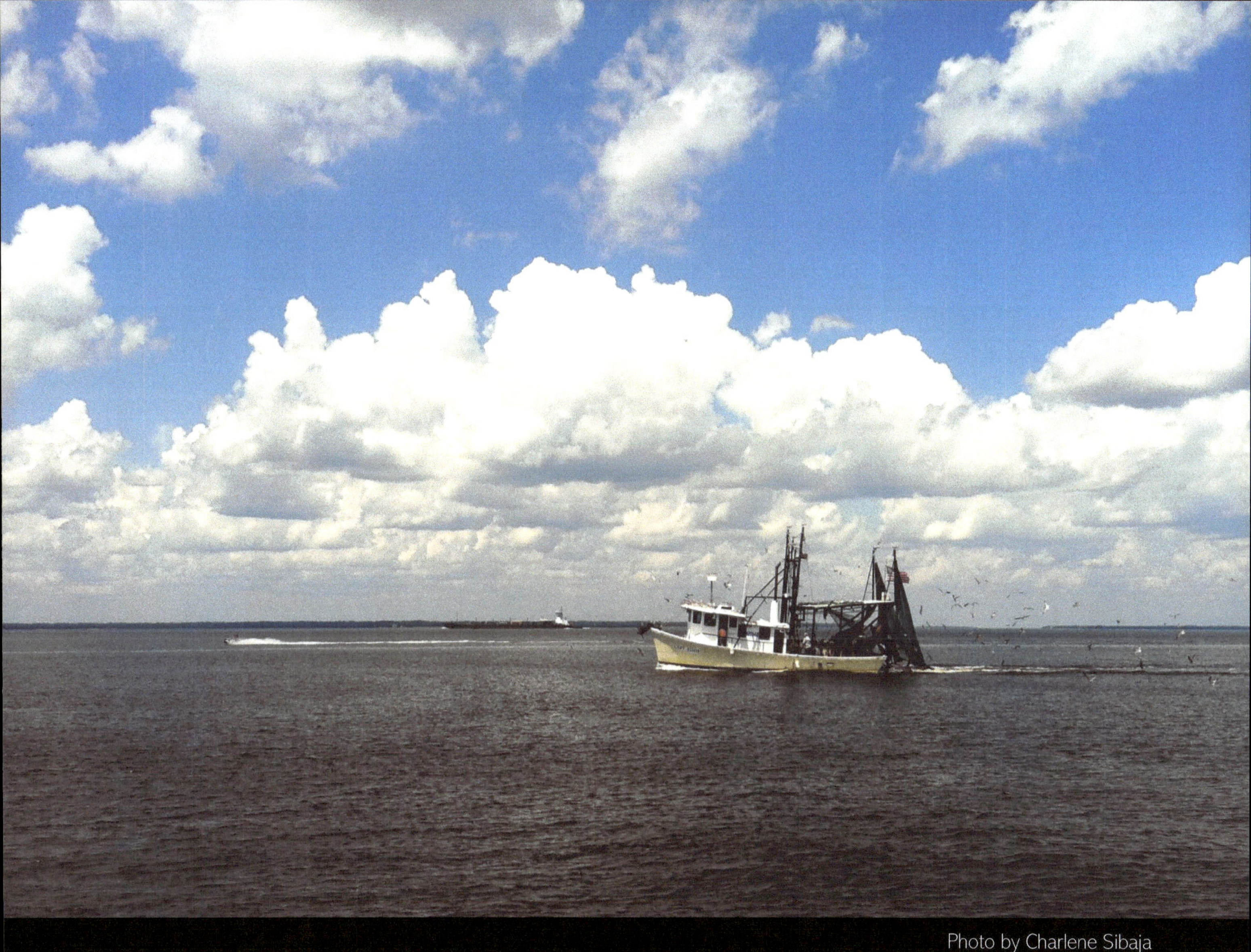
Photo by Charlene Sibaja

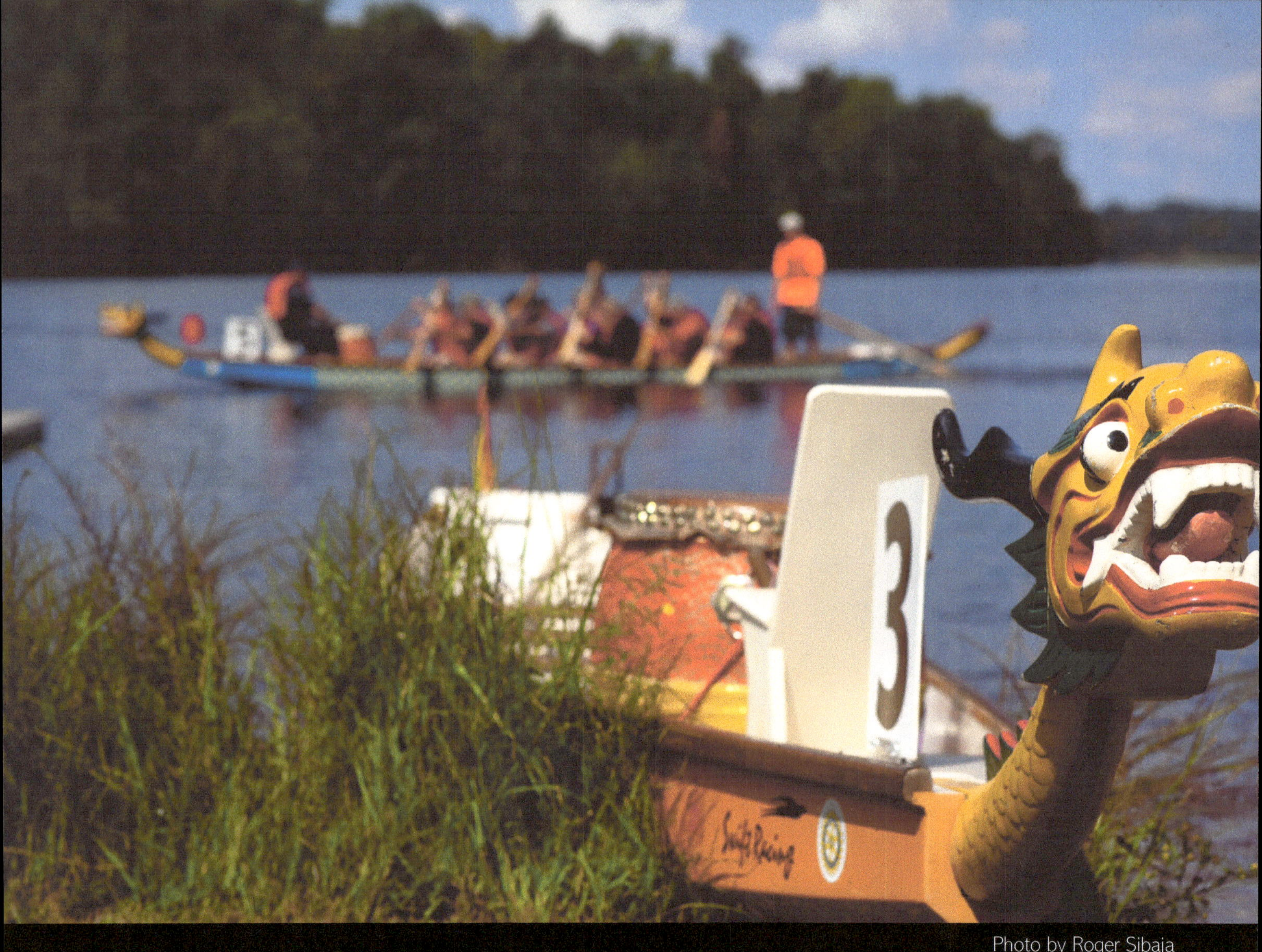

Photo by Roger Sibaja

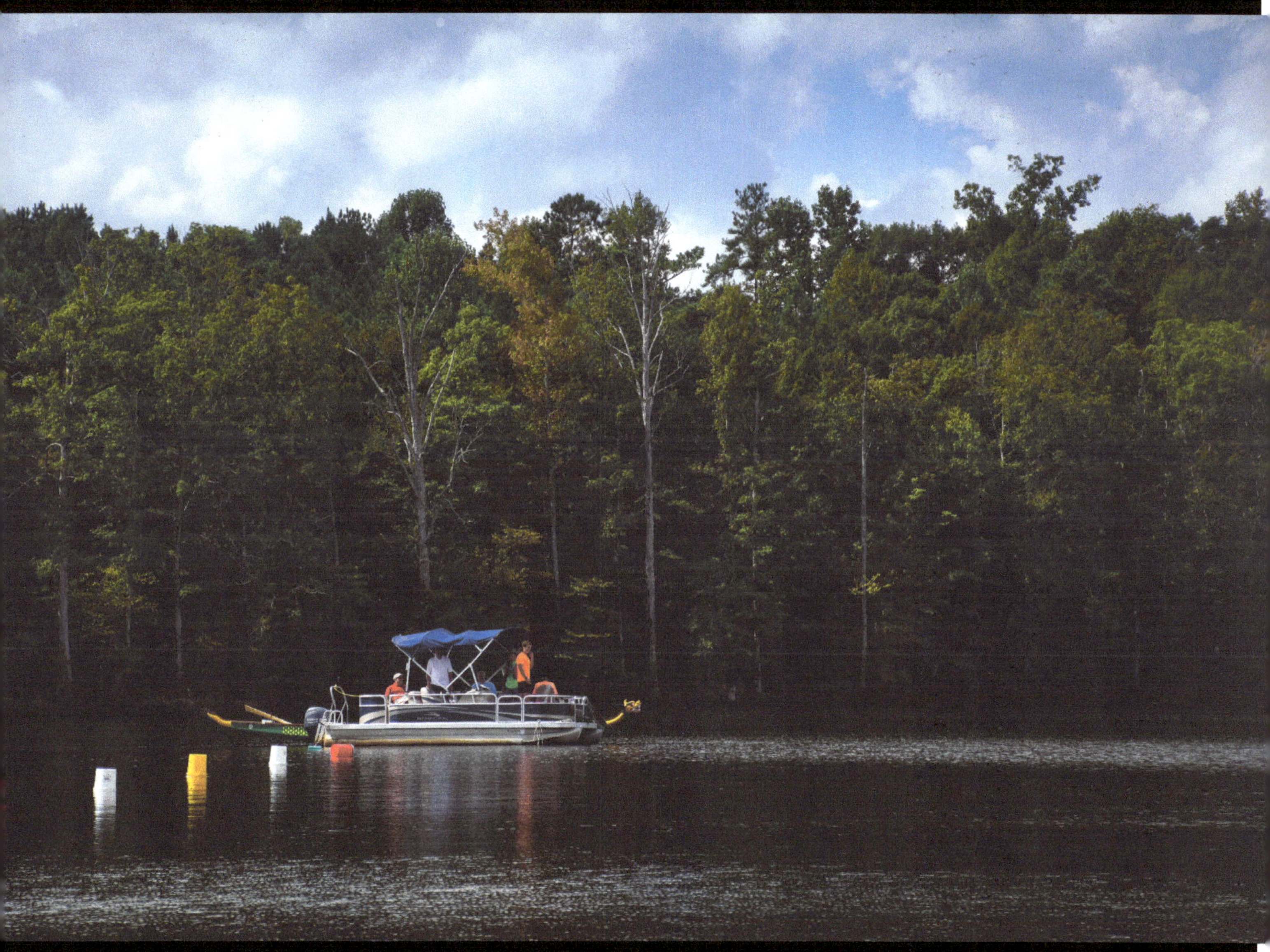

Photo by Charlene Sibaja

Playground Photographers

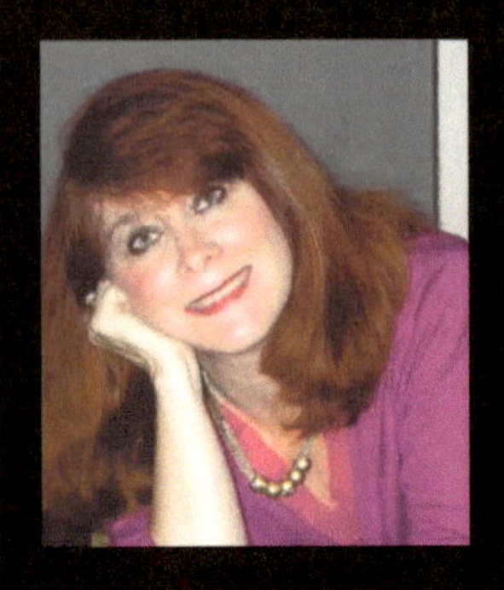

Lynn Murphy has a degree in Communications, English and Journalism from Mercer University as well as teaching credentials in Art and English. She is married and the mother of two sons. She lives in Peachtree City, Georgia and is the recipient of the Margot Stern Strom Teaching Award from Facing History and Ourselves.

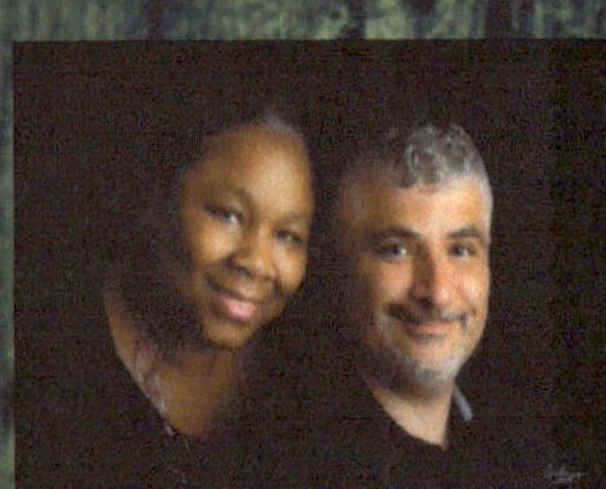

Roger and Charlene Sibaja are Gobi Photography. After spending years travelling the globe, they settled in Georgia and fell in love with photographing its rural scenes. As Gobi Photography, they published Discovering Scenes of Georgia: Mills, Bridges, Churches, Lighthouses and More. The book reached #1 in two categories on Amazon. Today, they run a

Playground Photographers

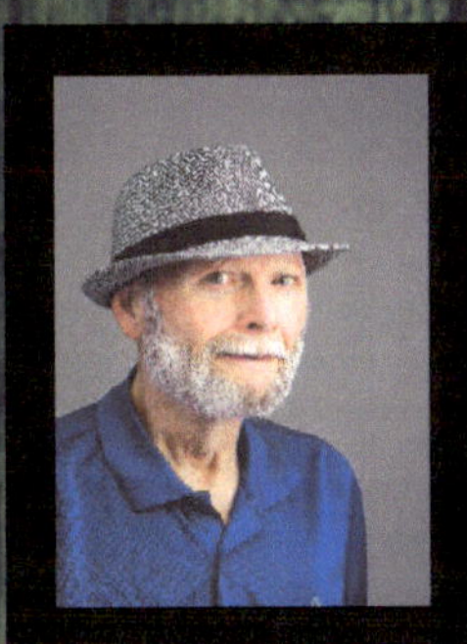

Hello, I am Jimmy Johns. Photography as an art form has intrigued me from the first Ansel Adams photo I saw till some 60 years later. My father was a photographer, I was exposed to many hours in the darkroom and walking the streets of our riverfront town. I quickly found my vision of the world was actuality the art I could see with just the click of the shutter and movement of the mouse across the screen. I could be Ansel Adams and Picasso all in one.

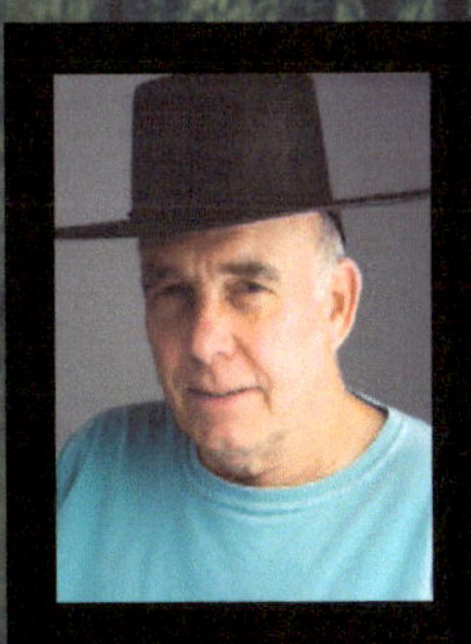

Randy Johnson a lifelong resident of Georgia has always enjoyed the outdoors. During his teen years, he would take photo's while exploring the world around him. In 2011 Randy bought his first DSLR. Wanting to improve he read numerous books on digital photography. After retiring in 2014 Randy was able to spend more time with his camera and friends taking images. He enjoys taking photos of wildlife and landscapes in remote areas.

Playground Photographers

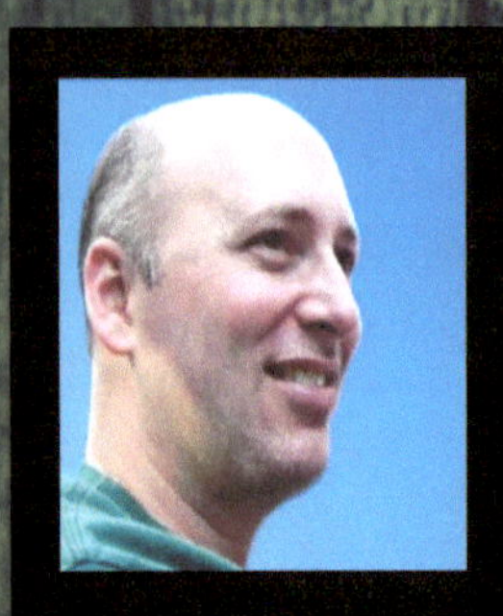

Hi! I'm Jeff Clough. I discovered photography several years ago and have been honing both my technical and artistic skill. I'm concentrating now on working with professional models and portrait subjects to capture and express personality and to evoke attitudes and emotion in the viewer. I really enjoy the "time machine" aspect of event photography, and the way it lets me capture relationships in a little time capsule.

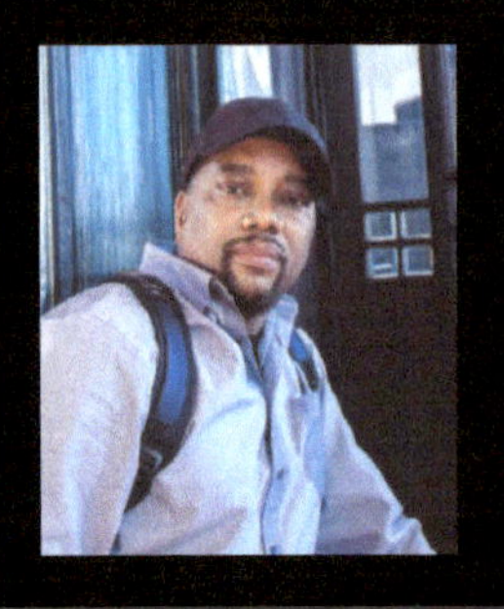

Hello, my name is Paul Taliferro Jr. I'm the founder or Upskale Multimedia. which is my video, photography and multimedia company. Originally from New York City and move to Virginia early on. Now reside in Atlanta GA. I'm a self-taught photographer. I'm a published photographer: my work has been seen in several magazines as well as book covers.

Did you like what you saw?

Photos from this book are available for sale

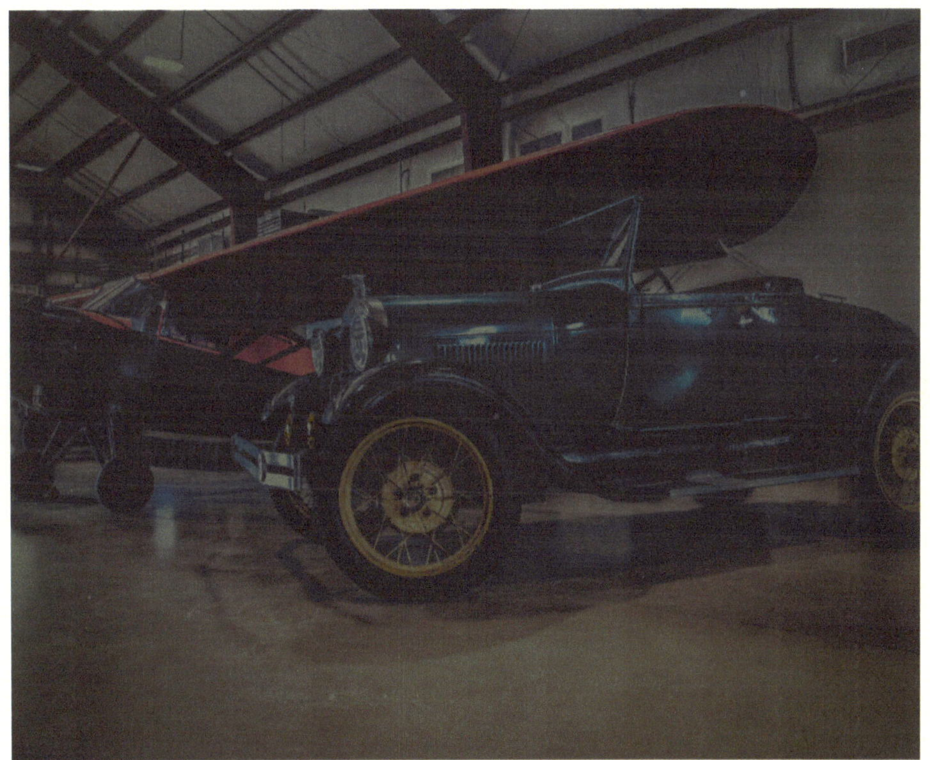

For pricing and ordering information email info@photographersplayground.com

www.ingramcontent.com/pod-product-compliance
Lightning Source LLC
LaVergne TN
LVHW070219110826
845147LV00003B/611

* 9 7 8 1 9 4 8 4 7 9 0 1 1 *